Galatians

The Treasures of Liberty

Galatians

The Treasures of Liberty

Dr. Bo Wagner

Word of His Mouth Publishers
Mooresboro, NC

All Scripture quotations are taken from the **King James Version** of the Bible.

ISBN: 978-1-941039-35-9
Printed in the United States of America
©2023 Dr. Bo Wagner

Word of His Mouth Publishers
Mooresboro, NC
www.wordofhismouth.com

Table of Contents

Introduction To Galatians

There are some things that, if you saw them anywhere, but especially in a church, you would surely find them problematic at the very least.

Picture, if you will, a church member, unquestionably saved, arriving in church one Sunday morning wearing the oddest of things, chain gang apparatus. Shackles and chains on the legs, shackles and chains on the wrists, a chain joining the chain on the hands and the chain on the feet, and a heavy, six-foot chain with a heavy steel ball being dragged behind the person wearing all of this.

Mind you, he is not in an orange prison-issued jumpsuit; he is wearing church clothes like anyone else. And yet right along with his Sunday finest, he has all of those chains and all of that weight dragging him down as he makes his way into the sanctuary.

Naturally, someone would most assuredly ask him what was going on. And in this case, the conversation would go something like this.

Concerned Christian: "Hey brother, what's with the hardware? Did you kill somebody?"

Believer in shackles: "No, no, nothing like that."

Concerned Christian: "What then? Wait, wait, let me guess. You robbed a bank, didn't you?"

Believer in shackles: "Of course not!"

Concerned Christian: "Well then, what are you all tangled up in this chain for? It has to be something pretty serious. I bet you got caught dealing drugs, didn't you?"

Believer in shackles: "Don't be ridiculous; I wouldn't know cocaine from cough drops!"

Concerned Christian: "Well, look, there has to be some reason for you to be dragging around all these chains. I mean, look at you; you can hardly walk right under all the weight. So, how did you get like this?"

Believer in shackles, pointing to some relative newcomers in the church: "They told me I had to wear this stuff."

Concerned Christian: "Excuse me?"

Believer in shackles: "Those guys came by with this yoke of bondage and told me I had to wear it from now on."

Concerned Christian: "And you listened to them?"

Believer in shackles: "Well, they said it was for my own good!"

Concerned Christian: "Brother, let me ask you something. Are you better off now, bound in these chains, than you were before when you were free?"

Believer in shackles: "Well, no. Actually, these chains kind of hurt, and since I've been carrying them, I've been tired all the time."

Concerned Christian: "Then take them off."

Believer in shackles: "Can I do that?"

Concerned Christian: "Yes, you can. There's not one reason in the world for you to be enslaved. The choice is yours. If you want to be free, just take that chain off and refuse to wear it ever again."

Believer in shackles, after a long pause: "I will. I don't need this chain anymore."

That would be a story with a happy ending. But it would also be a story with an infuriating beginning. And that is a very good picture of what Paul was dealing with when he wrote the precious book of Galatians somewhere around A.D. 52 - A.D. 58. Let me show you the key verse in the book, and we will refer to it often in this study.

Galatians 5:1 *Stand fast therefore in the liberty wherewith Christ hath made us free, and be not entangled again with the yoke of bondage.*

The church at Galatia was a group of people who had been won to God by Paul. They had once been heathens bound in chains of sin, then became proselytes to Judaism and were bound under the law, exhausted by the weight of all of the commands of the elders. Then the best thing imaginable happened; they got saved and stepped into the glorious freedom of Christ. But then later, they fell for it when the Judaizers came back by and told them that grace was not enough and that they needed to pick that yoke of bondage up and put it right back on. Paul wrote this letter to them to correct the error they had fallen into, to liberate them from the yoke they were needlessly wearing. That is why I will be calling our study of Galatians *The Treasures of Liberty.*

It is my hope that you will not only learn what each verse of Galatians means but also take it to heart and not let anyone rob you of your liberty in Christ.

Chapter One
The Apostle and the Amen

Galatians 1:1 *Paul, an apostle, (not of men, neither by man, but by Jesus Christ, and God the Father, who raised him from the dead;) 2 And all the brethren which are with me, unto the churches of Galatia: 3 Grace be to you and peace from God the Father, and from our Lord Jesus Christ, 4 Who gave himself for our sins, that he might deliver us from this present evil world, according to the will of God and our Father: 5 To whom be glory for ever and ever. Amen.*

The Apostle

Galatians 1:1 *Paul, an apostle, (not of men, neither by man, but by Jesus Christ, and God the Father, who raised him from the dead;)*

Paul wrote at least thirteen books of the New Testament. Some think that he wrote Hebrews, in which case it would be fourteen, though I do not hold to that belief. But just taking the thirteen that we know for a fact are his because he signed his name to them, you can see something that Paul knew he needed to get across. Nine out of the thirteen have a common word found in the introduction:

Romans 1:1 *Paul, a servant of Jesus Christ, called to be an **apostle**, separated unto the gospel of God,*

1 Corinthians 1:1 *Paul, called to be an* **apostle** *of Jesus Christ through the will of God, and Sosthenes our brother,*

2 Corinthians 1:1 *Paul, an* **apostle** *of Jesus Christ by the will of God, and Timothy our brother, unto the church of God which is at Corinth, with all the saints which are in all Achaia:*

Galatians 1:1 *Paul, an* **apostle**, *(not of men, neither by man, but by Jesus Christ, and God the Father, who raised him from the dead;)*

Ephesians 1:1 *Paul, an* **apostle** *of Jesus Christ by the will of God, to the saints which are at Ephesus, and to the faithful in Christ Jesus:*

Colossians 1:1 *Paul, an* **apostle** *of Jesus Christ by the will of God, and Timotheus our brother,*

1 Timothy 1:1 *Paul, an* **apostle** *of Jesus Christ by the commandment of God our Saviour, and Lord Jesus Christ, which is our hope;*

2 Timothy 1:1 *Paul, an* **apostle** *of Jesus Christ by the will of God, according to the promise of life which is in Christ Jesus,*

Titus 1:1 *Paul, a servant of God, and an* **apostle** *of Jesus Christ, according to the faith of God's elect, and the acknowledging of the truth which is after godliness;*

In nine out of thirteen letters, Paul reminded the recipients that he was an apostle. That is from the Greek word *apostelos*, which means "One who has been sent out with a message." The idea is that the one doing the talking or the writing is not doing so under his own authority but under the authority of another and that the message is not his own idea but is the direct words of another. In all nine of the passages above, Paul says that he has been sent as an apostle by Jesus Christ! His authority was given to him by Jesus. His message was given to him by Jesus. On that basis, and on that basis alone, Paul expected to be obeyed.

The position of an apostle has come and gone; it was only for a short time. But the still extant position of the pastor or preacher must have the exact same basis. Our authority must come from Jesus, and our message must come from Jesus, and it is only on that basis that any preacher can rightfully expect to be obeyed! If a preacher cannot, rightfully dividing Scripture, point back to the written Word that Jesus gave us, and say, "We are going to do things this way because of this verse," then that man has no right to expect people to blindly follow him! Either by direct precept or at least by divine principle, a minister's authority must always come from the Bible.

Here is a real danger in the ministry. Preachers stand up to preach and teach week after week; they are seen and heard by all. They are the voice of authority. Because of that, people often end up believing things just because they say them. And if you think that is a good thing, you are very wrong! At a revival meeting in my area a few years back, an evangelist stood up and said, "You better never ever question one single thing the man of God says. If he says it, it's right, period."

When he said it, three thoughts immediately popped into my mind. One, the Bible is inspired, not the preacher. Two, what happens when this pastor dies and another one comes in that teaches heresy? Three, what about all the visitors who are there from the Seventh Day Adventists, the Catholic Church, and the Church of Christ, or maybe even from the local mosque?

Saying something like that is not only dumb, it is dangerous. Paul never one time said, "Follow me because of who I am." Instead, he said in so many words, "Follow me because of Who has sent me, and because I am giving you His words, not mine."

This is why every time a preacher preaches, his message needs to be loaded with Bible and Biblically accurate. Only then can a preacher like Paul tell people to follow him because he has been sent by Jesus Christ, and his message is from Jesus Christ.

Never settle for anything less than a preacher that can back up everything he says, does, and believes with Scripture! It may not be anywhere near as flashy and exciting as a situation in which someone knows how to work the crowd and consistently whip them into a frenzy, but it will help you to grow, it will ground you in the truth, and it will keep you out of trouble.

Notice that in our text, right after he called himself an apostle, Paul further elaborated by saying that his apostleship was not "of men or by man." And that brings us to another important thing to take note of. As you study the New Testament, you see that men of God are sent out by the local church, but they are called by God:

Acts 13:1 *Now there were in the church that was at Antioch certain prophets and teachers; as Barnabas, and Simeon that was called Niger, and Lucius of Cyrene, and Manaen, which had been brought up with Herod the tetrarch, and Saul.* **2** *As they ministered to the Lord, and fasted, the Holy Ghost said, Separate me Barnabas and Saul for the work whereunto I have called them.* **3** *And when they had fasted and prayed, and laid their hands on them, they sent them away.*

The commissioning came through the local church, but the calling came from God. And it is that calling part that Paul is focused on here. It was his design in saying, "Not of men or by man," to let the Galatians know that he was not "man called." The call to the ministry must come directly from God! I have been in the ministry for a very long time now. And I have never seen a mother-called preacher, or a preacher-called preacher, or a well-meaning church member-called preacher, or a self-called preacher end up as anything other than a disaster of a preacher.

There are a lot of dark, hard times in the ministry. Please do not misunderstand me; I love the ministry, and I have it good. But even in the best of ministries, there are some lonely nights and some soul-searching valleys. There are some times when you would to God He had called someone, anyone but you. And

14

in those times, the mother who called you will not be able to help. In those times, the preacher who called you will not be able to help. In those times, the well-meaning church member who called you will not be able to help. The only real help you will get in such times is from God, and you will only get that help from God if He is the one that actually called you! If God in heaven is looking down and saying, "What is that guy doing in the ministry? I never called him!" then you are in for trouble when the hard times hit.

I love it when young men are truly called into the ministry. That is a good reason to do it. But let me give you some bad reasons to go into the ministry.

"I can't do anything else" is a bad reason to go into the ministry. If you are going into the ministry because you cannot do plumbing or carpentry and you do not know how to wire an outlet, and you didn't do well enough in school to be a doctor or a lawyer, I promise you, you are going to be just as big a failure in the ministry as you were at everything else! God does not look down from heaven and say, "Oh, Look! There's a guy with no job skills whatsoever and no motivation to learn. I'll call him."

All of the men that Jesus Himself called into the ministry were men who could have done other things. In fact, they already were doing other things! They were fishermen and government workers and businessmen.

"I want people to like me" is another terrible, no good, very bad reason! A person who goes into the ministry on that basis may as well fall off the top bunk bed onto a concrete floor because, either way, he is in for a rude awakening!

The only good reason to go into the ministry is because God Himself reached down from heaven and gripped your heart in a vise and would not let go until you surrendered to the gospel ministry.

The Audience

Galatians 1:2 *And all the brethren which are with me, unto the churches of Galatia:*

It is in this second verse of the book that we find its intended audience.

Galatia was a province of Asia Minor, having Pontus on the east, Bithynia and Paphlagonia north, Cappadocia and Phrygia to the south, and Phrygia to the west. (Lindner, Barnes) This region included cities like Pisidia, Lycaonia, Iconium, Derbe, Lystra, and Antioch of Pisidia. It was in what is now modern-day Turkey. This was a region that Paul was very familiar with because he had been there. In fact, the last six cities I just mentioned are cities in which Paul preached the gospel and was then persecuted for it. (Pfeifer, 209)

The very first time the region of Galatia is mentioned by name in Scripture, it is in reference to the missionary journeys of the Apostle Paul:

Acts 16:6 *Now when they had gone throughout Phrygia and the region of Galatia, and were forbidden of the Holy Ghost to preach the word in Asia,* **7** *After they were come to Mysia, they assayed to go into Bithynia: but the Spirit suffered them not.*

Paul and company went throughout the region of Galatia, preaching, winning souls, and establishing churches. After a time, he came through again:

Acts 18:23 *And after he had spent some time there, he departed, and went over all the country of Galatia and Phrygia in order, strengthening all the disciples.*

So from these two references, we know that the audience of this book was a group of people who had been won to the Lord by Paul, trained by Paul, and then later visited again and further established by him. In other words, this was a group of people and a group of churches that should have been rock solid and unmovable in the faith. But baby Christians are often frustratingly easy targets for false doctrine. Since the devil can no longer get their souls, his attack then turns to getting their minds and getting them off into error that will ruin their effectiveness for the Lord.

That is the exact approach the devil took with the churches of Galatia. The audience of this book was a bunch of baby Christians who were being seduced by false doctrine that was going to enslave them in a yoke. We start to see that in Galatians 1:7, and it progresses in great detail as you go through the book. The enemy was a group of people called Judaizers, and Paul names them as such in Galatians 2:14, using the word *judaidzo* for the word Jew.

These people were teaching that grace was not enough and that our works must be added to God's grace in order for us to truly be saved. And in some subtle ways, it even extended to teaching that even if people were saved, they could not really be classified as holy unless they added extra-Biblical works and traditions to salvation.

We will cover that in great detail throughout the book. For now, just know that type of Judaizing mentality has not gone away; it has just changed labeling through the years. No one is telling us to sacrifice lambs and wear only single-fabric clothing anymore, but any time anyone tells you that you need to add something to the blood of Jesus to be saved, it is just Judaism repackaged.

"You have to be baptized to be saved," says the Church of Christ. And that is Judaizing repackaged, trying to enslave men in a yoke of bondage.

"You must worship on Saturday, or you have taken the mark of the beast," says the Seventh Day Adventists. And that is Judaizing repackaged, trying to enslave men in a yoke of bondage.

"You must pray the rosary and venerate Mary and be confirmed and take the mass," says the Catholic Church. And that is Judaizing repackaged, trying to enslave men in a yoke of bondage.

But as I mentioned, there is another subtle form that this Judaizing takes. When they cannot convince men that they have to have these works to be saved, they then try to convince men that they need to adopt their non-biblical preferences to be truly holy. The first undermines a right understanding of salvation; the second undermines a right understanding of sanctification.

Let me state at this point that there is a bit of a subtle difference between Judaizing and legalism, though they are incredibly similar and often intertwined. Legalism is mentioned very often in Christian circles, usually when people are arguing about something. The word itself is not found in the Bible, but from the principles found in the Bible, it is accurately defined as any attempt to add works to grace for salvation. And the Judaizers were absolutely guilty of that.

But you can also look through many places in the New Testament and find the second thing I mentioned, the desire to convince people that they need to adopt non-biblical preferences to be truly holy, things that are taught neither directly by precept nor even indirectly by accurately applied divine principle. Paul dealt with that extensively throughout his writings and throughout his interactions with people. That does not technically fall under the commonly accepted definition of legalism, though some people term it as such. But it did present a problem, and it does always need to be dealt with when it arises. Here are just a few instances that I have personally encountered through the years.

"You need to get the stringed instruments out of your church. It does not matter that the Bible mentions them over and over; you need to get rid of them because we don't like them." That is the subtler form of Judaizing repackaged, trying to enslave men in a yoke of bondage.

"You need to be quiet. Shouting and praising may be spoken of more than eight hundred times in Scripture, but we don't like it, so be quiet, or you can't really be holy." That is the subtler form of Judaizing repackaged, trying to enslave men in a yoke of bondage.

On the flip side, there is "If you do not shout the house down, you are not really holy." That is the subtler form of Judaizing repackaged, trying to enslave men in a yoke of bondage.

"Don't ever use technology in your church. Hymn books are holy (as long as the cover is red), but when you put those exact same words up on a screen, it becomes unholy!" That is the subtler form of Judaizing repackaged, trying to enslave men in a yoke of bondage.

"Stop laughing and smiling. You're not supposed to enjoy going to church. Don't ever tell a joke from the pulpit. Let's be serious." That is the subtler form of Judaizing repackaged, trying to enslave men in a yoke of bondage.

"Trailer hitches are idols." (No, I am not making that up). That is the subtler form of Judaizing repackaged, trying to enslave men in a yoke of bondage.

"Only harlots wear lipstick." That is the subtler form of Judaizing repackaged, trying to enslave men in a yoke of bondage.

I have heard hundreds of other examples. And none of it is Biblical. It is just the subtler form of Judaizing repackaged, trying to enslave men in a yoke of bondage. And it is not really necessary to quibble over semantics. Whether one calls it legalism or Judaizing, it is still wrong and harmful. Again, if something can be proven from Scripture either by direct command or by accurately applied divine principle, then it should be obeyed without hesitation. But if it is nothing more than a preference, even an incredibly strong preference, then you are welcome to it—you are just not welcome to force it on others.

The audience that Paul was writing to could relate to this mentality. Both in matters of salvation and sanctification, they had been invaded by people that desperately wanted to steal their freedom and enslave them once more.

The Amen

Galatians 1:3 *Grace be to you and peace from God the Father, and from our Lord Jesus Christ, 4 Who gave himself for our sins, that he might deliver us from this present evil world, according to the will of God and our Father: 5 To whom be glory for ever and ever. Amen.*

Paul ended his introduction with a great word, Amen! It means, "So be it; I agree!" When you say amen, you are agreeing to and even rejoicing over what has been said. That is why even though I enjoy saying amen, I am also careful about saying amen. If I am going to say amen, I am going to understand what is being said, and it is going to be something I agree with. I hate being a spoilsport, but there have been times I have gotten caught in a meeting where a guy was way out on a limb, sawing it off behind him, and to shore himself up, he was constantly saying, "Say amen right there!" I am sorry, but I am not saying amen unless it is warranted.

In this case, there was some meat behind the amen. This introduction that Paul gave in the Epistle to Galatia is rich! It really does set the stage for everything that follows in the book and for Paul's assertion that we should not be wearing any yoke.

Verse three gives the first reason for the amen, and it is the fact that God the Father and God the Son have gone together to give us two very precious things—grace and peace.

Grace is the first thing that Paul told the Galatians they could and should say amen to. Grace is "God's unmerited favor." It is "God's riches at Christ's expense." It is "God giving us what we do not deserve." The Greek word *xaris* that it comes from indicates that which brings delight, joy, loveliness, pleasure, sweetness, and charm.

Those are general definitions. Here are some specifics:

Grace is God the Father and God the Son looking through time before the world ever was, seeing the mess that we would make if they created us, and making us anyway. Grace is the fact that before there ever was an Eden, God had decided that there would also be a Calvary. Grace is the fact that before there ever was an accuser of the brethren, Jesus determined to be our advocate with the Father.

Thank God, and Amen for grace!

The second thing Paul said amen over was peace. The world cannot seem to understand that in our lost estate, we are the enemies of God, not the children of God. Someone had to make peace, and the only one that could do it was the stronger of the two parties. The weaker party can ask for peace, but only the stronger party can make peace. And thank God He did:

Romans 5:1 *Therefore being justified by faith, we have peace with God through our Lord Jesus Christ:*

The lost world did not even have the sense to ask for peace. But God loved us enough to offer it to us and make it possible through the blood of His own Son.

Verse four gives the next set of reasons why Paul could and we should say amen:

Galatians 1:4 *Who gave himself for our sins, that he might deliver us from this present evil world, according to the will of God and our Father:*

This was a direct reference to the cross of Calvary.

Paul said here that the reason for that sacrifice on Calvary was so that God could "deliver us from this present evil world." It was not then, nor is it now, nor will it ever be God's desire for us to fit in with this present evil world. It is His desire to deliver us from it. That is why when we get saved, He calls us to unite with a local church. The word church is from the Greek word *ekklesia*, and it means a "called out assembly."

The world cannot seem to get this.

A few years ago, a particularly snippy radio talk show host was ripping into the North Carolina Baptist Association for removing Myers Park Baptist Church over accepting unrepentant homosexuals into membership. He said, "Yeah, that's what Jesus did; He died on the cross so we could exclude sinners from the church."

He does not get it. Salvation is not so the sinner can feel good about their sin; salvation is so the sinner can be redeemed from their sin. The church is a place where people who have been redeemed from their sins can meet together to worship the one who redeemed them from their sins. I love it when sinners come to church. We want them to come so that they can hear the gospel and get saved. But we are not going to win any of them by telling them that Jesus died on Calvary so that they can be free to live however they want. No, Jesus died on Calvary so that He could deliver us *from* this present evil world, not to make us at home *in* this present evil world.

Is this my will? Is it Paul's will? Is it the will of some Baptist Fellowship? No, according to verse four, this is the direct will of God and our Father.

Verse five gives us an idea of what God deserves based on what He has done:

Galatians 1:5 *To whom be glory for ever and ever...*

Glory is from the word *doxa*, and it means brightness, shining, praise. In other words, shine the brightest light possible on what Jesus has done! When we understand what He has done, our logical conclusion is, "Amen! I agree! God, you really do deserve all glory and honor and power! You have offered us grace and peace; You have given Yourself for our sins that we might be delivered from this present evil world; You deserve all glory forever and ever, amen!"

This is what God has done for us. And you can either live in the light of it, or you can allow some man somewhere to put you in a yoke and steal the joy that is your birthright as a child of God.

As we get further into this book, you are going to meet the Judaizers, who were intent on loading people down with their own rules and traditions and customs. Paul was furious at the very thought of it. And we should be as well because it still goes on even in our day. The Judaizers haven't left; they have just changed uniforms over the years. You can either listen to them and wear the yoke, or you can listen to the apostle and say amen right along with him and leave the yoke behind.

I, for one, will not wear the yoke.

Chapter Two
Heteros Allos: Things That Are Different Are Not the Same

Galatians 1:6 *I marvel that ye are so soon removed from him that called you into the grace of Christ unto another gospel: 7 Which is not another; but there be some that trouble you, and would pervert the gospel of Christ. 8 But though we, or an angel from heaven, preach any other gospel unto you than that which we have preached unto you, let him be accursed. 9 As we said before, so say I now again, If any man preach any other gospel unto you than that ye have received, let him be accursed. 10 For do I now persuade men, or God? or do I seek to please men? for if I yet pleased men, I should not be the servant of Christ. 11 But I certify you, brethren, that the gospel which was preached of me is not after man. 12 For I neither received it of man, neither was I taught it, but by the revelation of Jesus Christ.*

In the first five verses, we learned about "The Apostle and the Amen." Paul reminded the beleaguered Galatians where his authority and message came from and gave them some glorious things to shout about, namely the grace and peace that Jesus gives. We will cover verses six through twelve in this chapter.

A Difference

Galatians 1:6 *I marvel that ye are so soon removed from him that called you into the grace of Christ unto another gospel: 7 Which is not another; but there be some that trouble you, and would pervert the gospel of Christ.*

When Paul said that he *marveled* at the Galatians, it is from the Greek word *thaumadzo*, and it indicates two things— surprise and sorrow. Paul was both surprised and saddened that these dear folks that he had won to God had fallen prey to false doctrine that had stripped them of their freedom in Christ and had enslaved them once again.

There are times when someone makes a profession of faith, and we suspect right off the bat that there is not much reality to their profession. But then there are times when you have been watching someone for weeks; they have obviously been under deep conviction, and they finally come broken to the altar and make a profession of faith. For years after, they live right, they are on fire for God, and they hold pure doctrine.

But sometimes, you get word that those who have been so solid for so long have changed completely and have gone off into abject doctrinal heresy, and it just makes your jaw drop. And that is much like what Paul was experiencing; people he had confidence in had gone bad in their doctrine. But in this case, it had not taken many years; it had all happened rather quickly.

Surprise is the first aspect of the word marvel; sadness is the second. It is very easy to get mad when people forsake sound doctrine, and Paul was angry, but he was also saddened. You see, whenever anyone goes off into false doctrine, people get hurt. When that happens, let your anger be directed at the false teacher and your sorrow at the one who has fallen prey to it. This is just how Paul demonstrated it. When a person or group is teaching deadly error, we need to get furious in a hurry. But when a baby Christian is getting infected, we need to be stern with them if need be, but surprised and sorrowful as well.

What Paul was so amazed at was that the Galatians had been *"so soon removed from him that called you into the grace of Christ unto another gospel."* They fell for grievous error, and it did not even take long!

And now let us focus on that word *another* for a moment; it is essential to what Paul was saying. The word *another* in verse six is from the word *heteros*. You may recognize it whether you realize it yet or not. A *Hetero*sexual is one who is attracted to members of a sex that is completely different from their own. The Greek word *heteros* means "another of a different kind." Keep that in mind, and then look at verse seven:

Galatians 1:7 *Which is not another; but there be some that trouble you, and would pervert the gospel of Christ.*

The first word for *another* was *heteros*, another of a different kind. The "gospel" that the Judaizers were preaching was not like the one that Paul was preaching; it was completely different.

When you get to the *another* of verse seven, Paul does not use the word *heteros*. This time he uses the word *allos*. That word for *another* means another of the same kind. So when you put those two words in those two verses together, here is what you have:

Galatians 1:6 *I marvel that ye are so soon removed from him that called you into the grace of Christ unto another gospel* [of a completely different kind]*: 7 Which is not another* [of the same kind].

That was Paul's very eloquent way of saying this: things that are different are not the same! No matter how small the change may be, things that are different are just not the same. Especially when you go tinkering with salvation, you are treading on dangerous ground because there is only one way, and the eternal souls of men and women and boys and girls are at stake! When you change the gospel, people are going to die and go to hell, and their blood will be on your hands. The gospel, the good news, is that Jesus died to save sinners, was buried, rose again three days later, and by His grace will save anyone who in faith turns from sin to Christ.

It is so beautiful and so simple. So why would anyone twist and pervert that gospel? Paul gives their motivation at the end of verse seven:

...but there be some that trouble you, and would pervert the gospel of Christ.

Their motivation was to pervert the gospel of Christ, and in so doing, they were "troubling" the Galatians. That word for pervert means to "turn completely around." It was not accidental; it was utterly intentional. These charlatans did not just want to "tweak" the gospel, as horrible as even that would have been; they wanted to give it a one-eighty! There was really nothing about grace that they liked at all. They liked the law. They liked their customs and traditions. They liked having people under their thumbs, and every time someone got saved, they slipped out from under their thumbs! This was all about control. Anytime anyone adds something to Scripture and demands that you live by it, it is always about control. The cults and the Pharisees do not want you to have the freedom that Christ gives; they want you to be beholden to them.

A Damnation

This matter of coming up with another gospel is something God takes very seriously. Look at the command he gave through Paul:

Galatians 1:8 *But though we, or an angel from heaven, preach any other gospel unto you than that which we have preached unto you, let him be accursed.*

Does that sound stern? Look at the next verse:

Galatians 1:9 *As we said before, so say I now again, If any man preach any other gospel unto you than that ye have received, let him be accursed.*

It sounds like God is repeating Himself because He is, and it is intentional. It is for extreme emphasis. No one, no man, no angel, no "apostle" is allowed to produce, preach, or propagate any other so-called "gospel." If they do, they are to be regarded as accursed. That is a Greek word that you are probably very familiar with because we use it in English as well. It is the word *anathema*. It means "doomed to destruction with no hope of being redeemed." That is as serious as it gets! That is the fate of anyone who decides that the gospel of Jesus Christ is not good enough, so they go out and produce and preach their own.

Look again at whom Paul mentions in regard to this: apostles, angels, or any man at all. That covers Moroni and the false gospel that was given to Joseph Smith, founder of the Mormons. It covers the slander that Gabriel gave Muhammad the blueprint for Islam. It covers every fallen angel; it covers every cult of supposed angelic origin. God covered all of the bases in these two very blunt verses. No matter who it is, angel, man, apostle, things that are different are not the same, and anyone who knowingly produces, preaches, and propagates another so-called gospel is anathema, condemned to destruction forever with no hope of being redeemed.

A Delight

Galatians 1:10 *For do I now persuade men, or God? or do I seek to please men? for if I yet pleased men, I should not be the servant of Christ.*

This verse and some other accusations that Paul alludes to throughout the book let us know a bit about the tactics of the Judaizers, and this will be important to remember throughout the whole book. They were trying to undermine the message by undermining the messenger. They were accusing Paul of doing what he did and saying what he said to please men. The word *persuade* is from the word *peitho* and means "to win someone's favor." It is another way of saying what he said twice in the remainder of the verse when he spoke of either *pleasing* man or being the servant of Christ. He knew that it was an either/or.

The Judaizers were saying that Paul could not be trusted because he was only interested in what people thought of him, and nothing could have been farther from the truth. The last two verses, verses eight and nine, effectively obliterate that idea; one does not please men by being that harsh and pointed!

The answer to the question in verse ten was abundantly clear. Paul was only interested in pleasing Christ, and because of that, he could be trusted to tell the truth. When a person is only delighted in pleasing God and gives no thought or attention to pleasing man, that person is likely to be one that you can trust.

A Distinction

Galatians 1:11 *But I certify you, brethren, that the gospel which was preached of me is not after man.* **12** *For I neither received it of man, neither was I taught it, but by the revelation of Jesus Christ.*

This is the only time the word certify is used in the New Testament. It means to make clearly known. In other words, what Paul said was something he wanted them to know beyond any shadow of a doubt. And this is what he wanted them to know: you can either get your message from God or from man, those are the only two options, and Paul got his message from God by the direct revelation of Jesus Christ.

What option did that leave for the Judaizers? If Paul's message came from God, theirs had to come from men. Paul was saying, "When I came, you accepted my message as being from God. But then, when the Judaizers showed up with a completely different message, you accepted their message as being from God too. That is impossible! Things that are different are not the same. They can't both be from God. You can't believe both them and me because we are saying different things."

The yoke that these Galatians were willingly submitting to was a man-made yoke of bondage! Anything but the gospel of the Lord Jesus Christ is nothing but a yoke of bondage, and wise people will refuse it outright.

———————————— ～——／————————————

For all of the thousands of religions in the world, there are really only two. There is Christianity, which tells you that you are helpless and in desperate need of a Savior to rescue you, and then there are all the rest, all of which tell you that if you just try hard enough, you will make it.

On December 5, 1986, Walter Wyatt, Jr. Climbed into his little Beechcraft airplane, took off from Nassau, Bahamas, and headed for Miami. Normally the flight only took him sixty-five minutes. But, a few days earlier, thieves had looted the navigational equipment in his Beechcraft. So on this day, Walter Wyatt Jr. was flying guided by just a compass and a hand-held radio. And shortly after takeoff, the skies were blackened by storm clouds.

When his compass began to gyrate, Walter concluded he was headed in the wrong direction. He flew his plane below the clouds, hoping to spot something, but soon he knew he was lost. He put out a Mayday call, which brought a Coast Guard Falcon search plane to lead him to an emergency landing strip only six miles away. But suddenly, Wyatt's right engine coughed its last and died. The fuel tank had run dry. Wyatt could do little more than glide the plane into the water. It was around 8:00 p.m.

Wyatt survived the crash, but his plane disappeared quickly, leaving him bobbing on the water in a leaky life vest. With blood on his forehead, Wyatt floated on his back. Suddenly he felt a hard bump against his body; a shark had found him. Wyatt kicked the intruder and wondered if he would survive the

31

night. He managed to stay afloat for the next ten hours. In the morning, Wyatt saw no airplanes, but in the water, a dorsal fin was headed for him. Twisting, he felt the hide of a shark brush against him. In a moment, two more bull sharks sliced through the water toward him. Again he kicked the sharks, and they veered away, but he was nearing exhaustion. Then he heard the sound of a distant aircraft. When it was within a half mile, he waved his orange vest. The pilot radioed the Cape York, which was twelve minutes away, "Get moving, cutter! There's a shark targeting this guy!" As the Cape York pulled alongside Wyatt, a Jacob's ladder was dropped over the side. Wyatt climbed wearily out of the water and onto the ship, where he fell to his knees and kissed the deck. Had it not been for a rescue boat, there is no way he would have survived, exhausted and bleeding in the water against the sharks that were determined to devour him. (Editors, 2022)

When the boat came by, Walter Wyatt did not say, "You guys go on your way. I'm sure you think your boat is the only way, but I'll just do things my own way." How foolish that would have been! That rescue boat was the only hope he had. And for every lost sinner across the world, the only hope is the old rescue ship of Zion, the gospel of Jesus Christ. It set sail from Calvary 2,000 years ago and has been snatching desperate souls out of certain destruction ever since.

And there will never be another option.

Chapter Three
Carefully Planned from Out of Nowhere

Galatians 1:13 *For ye have heard of my conversation in time past in the Jews' religion, how that beyond measure I persecuted the church of God, and wasted it:* **14** *And profited in the Jews' religion above many my equals in mine own nation, being more exceedingly zealous of the traditions of my fathers.* **15** *But when it pleased God, who separated me from my mother's womb, and called me by his grace,* **16** *To reveal his Son in me, that I might preach him among the heathen; immediately I conferred not with flesh and blood:* **17** *Neither went I up to Jerusalem to them which were apostles before me; but I went into Arabia, and returned again unto Damascus.* **18** *Then after three years I went up to Jerusalem to see Peter, and abode with him fifteen days.* **19** *But other of the apostles saw I none, save James the Lord's brother.* **20** *Now the things which I write unto you, behold, before God, I lie not.* **21** *Afterwards I came into the regions of Syria and Cilicia;* **22** *And was unknown by face unto the churches of Judaea which were in Christ:* **23** *But they had heard only, That he which persecuted us in times past now preacheth the faith which once he destroyed.* **24** *And they glorified God in me.*

Perspective really is an amazing thing. Let me illustrate that for you. Please take your index finger and lay the side of it flat against your nose, right between your eyes. What does it look like to you? It is sort of hard to tell, isn't it? It is so close that it is totally blurred. But to whoever is watching you right now, it looks crystal clear like a finger – and you look like an oddball.

Here is another illustration. How is it possible for an entire region to be totally engulfed in a storm with such a dark cloud cover that for hundreds and hundreds of miles, it looks like night even though it is day, but in that very same region are one hundred fifty or so people that are enjoying blue skies and bright sunshine? If you have ever been flying, you know the answer to that. Below the clouds, all is dark; above the clouds, all is bright and beautiful!

Galatians 1:13-24 gives us a good example of that kind of perspective. To everyone that looked on, the emergence of the apostle Paul had to seem like it came out of nowhere. He did not have the background of the other apostles. But verses fifteen and sixteen let us know that God had all of Paul's ministry planned before he was ever born.

Paul had written to the Galatians to tell them not to go back under a yoke of bondage. But while he was doing that, he had to defend himself because the Judaizers were attacking the messenger to undermine the message. A lot of this book is Paul telling about himself. The last half of chapter one is like that. This chapter examines the different perspectives on Paul himself.

The Past Life of Paul

Galatians 1:13 *For ye have heard of my conversation in time past in the Jews' religion, how that beyond measure I persecuted the church of God, and wasted it:* **14** *And profited in the Jews' religion above many my equals in mine own nation, being more exceedingly zealous of the traditions of my fathers.*

34

As this section begins, right off the bat, an interesting word appears. Paul reminded the Galatians that they had heard of his "conversation" in times past. When you hear the word conversation today, it almost invariably means speaking. But it meant a great deal more to the world in the day of Paul. The word *anastrophayn*, conversation, meant an entire manner of life! As far as they were concerned, you talked as much with the way you walk as with the way you talk! And in that, they had it right. Your words are not the real meat of your conversation. Your conduct is the real meat of your conversation.

A few years back, near the outskirts of North Carolina, at a Jubilee meeting, a pretty big-name preacher was the featured speaker. All of the messages were wonderful, powerfully delivered, truly moving. But somehow, walking into the guest house and finding him with a woman he was not married to, and I mean WITH a woman he was not married to, made all of his words ring very hollow.

Right words are horribly undermined by a wrong life. You can dress up and smile and carry a big Bible to church, but if you lose your temper and act like a witch or an ogre in your home, your children will not believe your words, but they will model your works.

Paul had a wrong life in the beginning; his "conversation" was wrong. Verse thirteen says that "beyond measure" he persecuted the church of God and wasted it. **Acts 22:4** says, "*And I persecuted this way <u>unto the death</u>, binding and delivering into prisons both men and women.*"

There was simply no way to calculate the damage that Paul did. There was no way to bring back those that he murdered, no way to undo all of the torture that he had subjected people to, no way to fix all that had been broken. This man was the bitterest enemy the church ever had.

There is a reason that Paul brought this up and what follows. His purpose was to prove that what he was now saying

35

was not of man since such a radical change in his life could only be made by God Himself. The Judaizers did not have the radical change in their life that Paul had in his. They had not met God; he had!

Galatians 1:14 *And profited in the Jews' religion above many my equals in mine own nation, being more exceedingly zealous of the traditions of my fathers.*

The word "equals" in this verse is a reference to those of the same general age as Paul. Those he should have been just about on the same level as in the Jewish religion, he had blown past them. He studied harder, worked harder, believed more firmly, and gave a greater effort than everyone else. And he was lost! As he himself put it, all of his zeal was for the traditions that had been handed down to him, not for God or for God's Word.

But that leads me to what should be an obvious observation: how sad is it when lost people have better character than saved people?

Child of God, do not ever let an unsaved person outwork you. Do not let them study harder, do not let them show up earlier, do not let them be more polite. Every day that you go to work, you are carrying the reputation of every born-again child of God with you. Make it good!

Paul rose through the ranks of Judaism faster than anyone could have imagined. He was the rising star of the religious elite of his day; he had a bright future in the eyes of man. That was the past life of Paul. But oh, how things changed.

The Pleasure of God

Galatians 1:15 *But when it pleased God, who separated me from my mother's womb, and called me by his grace,* **16a** *To reveal his Son in me, that I might preach him among the heathen...*

There is really no way to fathom all that pleases God. Honestly, many of the things that please God are often the things that different people would choke at the very thought of.

Think about Hosea and God being pleased at having the preacher marry the local prostitute.

Think about the fact that according to Isaiah 53, the brutal, awful, shameful crucifixion of Christ was something that "pleased" the Father. Do you see what I mean? A lot of times, the things that please God are the things that we who "know a lot better than God does" find very distasteful. Maybe that is why Isaiah had to remind us of the obvious:

Isaiah 55:8 *For my thoughts are not your thoughts, neither are your ways my ways, saith the LORD.* **9** *For as the heavens are higher than the earth, so are my ways higher than your ways, and my thoughts than your thoughts.*

This was certainly true of the call of Saul of Tarsus to the ministry. This is somebody that none of us would have dared to encourage to ministry in the least. But Paul said, "It pleased God to reveal His Son in me, call me, and send me to the Gentiles to preach." And this verse tells us that God had that plan in mind when Paul was still in his mother's womb! Just as God had a plan for Jeremiah in the womb, He had a plan for Paul in the womb. He has a plan for every child in the womb, which is one thing that makes abortion such an abomination in the sight of God.

"But Paul was wicked!" Of course, he was. That is why the end of verse fifteen tells us that his call was birthed out of grace. Anything good that God does for us or in us or with us is all pure grace.

This passage had something in it to make everybody mad. The Judaizers would hate the part about God calling Paul; the Saduccees would be livid over the idea that Jesus was able to call Paul since they believed that He was still dead since there was no such thing as a resurrection, and the Jews would be livid over the idea that God would send anyone to the heathen Gentiles.

Aren't you glad that God is in charge instead of man?

The Path of Preparation

Galatians 1:16b *...immediately I conferred not with flesh and blood:*

There is a fairly normal, orthodox way for men to get into the ministry. Saved young, in church since childhood. Called to preach at maybe fifteen or sixteen. A preacher takes him under his wing for a few years. Off to Bible college. Take a position as an assistant for a while. Then finally, accept the call to pastor.

That is normal, orthodox, and there is not one thing wrong with it. But that is just our idea of how it should be. It is not written anywhere in the Bible that everyone has to follow that exact same path. I believe it is a good path; I recommend it. But never think that anyone who does not follow that path is unqualified!

When my wife was in Bible college, she was told that if she stopped short of a four-year degree, she could never be used by God in the ministry. She got a two-year degree. She can be a stubborn woman when needed (and I love that about her).

It truly is a shame she has not been able to be used in the ministry, though. All she has done is help me found a church that has gone from nothing to a couple of hundred members, been a pastor's wife all of these years, been the church pianist for all these years, been the church secretary for all these years, personally won probably fifty people to the Lord during that time, taught a bunch of little girls music during that time, built the original church website, host one of the biggest and best annual ladies meetings in the entire southeast, and become a sought-after mentor for countless young preacher's wives.

It is truly a shame that she hasn't been able to be used in the ministry like the folks at her college told her.

Paul took an unorthodox path to the ministry. He said that when he got saved, "Immediately he conferred not with flesh and blood." In other words, the first thing he could have been expected to do was go take counsel from the men already regarded as being in charge over the ministry, but he did not.

Would there have been anything wrong with him doing that first? No. But was there anything wrong with him not doing that first? No. And years later, the fact that God had him do it that way was coming back to help him because he was contending with a bunch of Judaizers who had told the Galatians that Paul was "man called." I bet when Paul began the way he began, he had no clue why God had him do it the way he did it. But God knew why He was having him do it that way, He knew what Paul would face in his future ministry, and He was preparing him from day one to be able to deal with it.

Galatians 1:17 *Neither went I up to Jerusalem to them which were apostles before me; but I went into Arabia, and returned again unto Damascus.*

Paul said in the last verse that, in general, he had not conferred with flesh and blood. In this verse, he got more specific. When he was called, he did not head for Jerusalem to confer with the apostles, who were apostles before he was. He bypassed Jerusalem, went into Arabia, the desert, and then headed back for Damascus, which was in Syria. We are told only here of that trip into the desert; neither Paul nor God felt inclined to give us any further details of it. But we do know that it was decidedly outside of "normal Christian circles." Jerusalem is where, figuratively speaking, everyone in Christian circles was bowing to. Not Damascus, and certainly not Arabia.

How many preachers "bow" to Greenville, or to Hammond, or to Powell, or Oklahoma, or any other number of

Bible college towns? With all due respect, we put too much stock in people and places.

I love Bible college. I taught in one for sixteen years. But I am amazed by the blind loyalty that people often give to Bible colleges. God did not die for the Bible college; He died for the local church. God does not do His work on earth through the Bible college (though they certainly come alongside and help); He does it through the local church.

Respect is well and good. Give honor to whom it is due. Do not run people or places down without need. But do not bow any direction but to Calvary, and never get the idea that any man's ideas or methods are infallible, especially not a Bible college. God may not have you get into the ministry by way of Jerusalem Hammond, or Jerusalem Greenville, or Jerusalem Powell. God may not have you born into a family where you become a fourth-generation preacher. He may not have you come up through a church where your pastor is so well known that you have an easy road of it.

You who are not preachers but are still active servants in a church, you may not be a second or third-generation Christian. You may have once been on the wrong side of the law. You men may use to have been hippies, and you ladies may have been pot-smoking flower children. If you are now saved, washed in the blood of the Lamb, none of that matters so much as an ounce. It did not matter to Paul. It surely did not hinder his ministry. Just think about it! Whom would you have expected to do any more than the people who were Jesus' disciples for three and a half years, walking with Him, being taught directly by Him? But even though eleven out of twelve of them went on to have decent ministries, Paul, a man from as far outside that circle as you could get, outdid all of them put together. Your background is not what matters; your ability to wholly sell out to God and be willing even to endure a life full of persecution for Him is what will make the difference.

Galatians 1:18 *Then after three years I went up to Jerusalem to see Peter, and abode with him fifteen days.* **19** *But other of the apostles saw I none, save James the Lord's brother.*

After years in the ministry, Paul finally went to see Peter, and he saw James as well. That, by the way, is an encouraging reference. This James, the Lord's brother, back in John 7:4-5 so disbelieved Jesus that he tried to get Him, His own half-brother, killed. And now, here he is as an apostle of that same Jesus!

It is good for preachers to be acquainted with each other, and that is what the word "see" in this verse means. But we must remember that a preacher's call is not from man, and we really do not need preachers from other churches to approve of us.

We sent a young man to Utah to start a church. Another man from there called me and told me that he had been there for twenty years, Mormons could not be won to God, and that all I was going to do was split the few Baptists who were there. I told that man he ought to leave the field if he felt that way.

If we waited for everyone to approve of us, no good churches would ever be started because jealousy is a powerful thing.

Galatians 1:20 *Now the things which I write unto you, behold, before God, I lie not.* **21** *Afterwards I came into the regions of Syria and Cilicia;* **22** *And was unknown by face unto the churches of Judaea which were in Christ:*

Why would Paul have to say, "I lie not?" For two reasons. One, what he was telling them was the exact opposite of what the Judaizers had spread about him. Two, the path he took to the ministry was not like the one most others took! Paul was an enigma. He did things differently. Not necessarily better, not worse, but different. God didn't send him down the same path He sent others.

The Persecutor Turned Preacher

Galatians 1:23 *But they had heard only, That he which* **persecuted** *us in times past now* **preacheth** *the faith which once he destroyed.* **24** *And they glorified God in me.*

Look at the end result of what God did with Paul: Paul went from persecutor to preacher. That is as drastic a change as can possibly be made. And what a preacher! There has never been a greater church planter, or soul-winner, or Bible writer than Paul. But focus on this: as far as most people were concerned, Paul came from out of nowhere. That was their perspective. But as far as God was concerned, all that went into making Paul the apostle what he was, was carefully planned from the foundation of the world. Paul was *Carefully Planned From Out of Nowhere.*

I want you to take something practical from this. There is nothing wrong with taking the "orthodox path" to serving Him. The best possible thing that can ever happen is for everyone to get saved as a little child, be in church every time the doors are open, stay away from sin, and serve God for an entire lifetime.

But God may not choose to send you down the orthodox path! You may have gotten saved late; you may have been pulled out of a horrible pit of sin. If God has saved you, cleansed you, and called you, do not ever feel cheated or inferior. Do not ever believe it when people tell you that you cannot do it. If God has called you, and you have not disqualified yourself based on Scripture, then serve God with all your heart, soul, mind, zeal, and emotion, and never look back except to glorify Him for what He has done in you.

Chapter Four
Standing for Truth in the House of God

Galatians 2:1 *Then fourteen years after I went up again to Jerusalem with Barnabas, and took Titus with me also.* **2** *And I went up by revelation, and communicated unto them that gospel which I preach among the Gentiles, but privately to them which were of reputation, lest by any means I should run, or had run, in vain.* **3** *But neither Titus, who was with me, being a Greek, was compelled to be circumcised:* **4** *And that because of false brethren unawares brought in, who came in privily to spy out our liberty which we have in Christ Jesus, that they might bring us into bondage:* **5** *To whom we gave place by subjection, no, not for an hour; that the truth of the gospel might continue with you.* **6** *But of these who seemed to be somewhat, (whatsoever they were, it maketh no matter to me: God accepteth no man's person:) for they who seemed to be somewhat in conference added nothing to me:* **7** *But contrariwise, when they saw that the gospel of the uncircumcision was committed unto me, as the gospel of the circumcision was unto Peter;* **8** *(For he that wrought effectually in Peter to the apostleship of the circumcision, the same was mighty in me toward the Gentiles:)* **9** *And when James, Cephas, and John, who seemed to be pillars, perceived the grace that was given unto me, they gave to me and Barnabas the right hands of* *fellowship; that we should go unto the heathen, and they unto the circumcision.* **10** *Only they would that we should remember the poor; the same which I also was forward to do.*

It seems almost counterintuitive, but one of the places most often in need of someone to stand up and stand for the truth is the church itself. Paul understood that and did not hesitate to oblige when necessary. And in these verses, we find a situation in which it was very, very necessary.

A Showdown in Jerusalem

Galatians 2:1 *Then fourteen years after I went up again to Jerusalem with Barnabas, and took Titus with me also.*

The fourteen years Paul is speaking about in this verse is referring back to Paul's own conversion that he told the Galatians about in chapter one. Paul told them that right after he got saved, instead of heading to Jerusalem as people might expect, he headed out into the desert of Arabia and then into Damascus. Sometime after that, he did go into Jerusalem for a few days and met with Peter. Then fourteen years after his conversion, after doing amazing missionary work, traveling the world, and winning heathen Gentiles to God, Paul headed into Jerusalem on official business, and he took two very significant people with him as he did.

One was Barnabas. Barnabas came onto the scene in Acts 4. He was from the Island of Cyprus, and when Pentecost took place and thousands of Christians almost overnight made Jerusalem their home, Barnabas sold land that he owned and gave the money to the apostles so they could give it to these needy saints. For doing that, he earned the name "the Son of Consolation."

Barnabas was the one who took Paul under his wings right after he got saved. None of the Christians trusted him, mostly because Paul (then known as Saul) had spent so much time killing or imprisoning them. Barnabas, though, did trust him, and he is the one that helped Paul get started in the ministry. People began to trust Paul because they already trusted Barnabas; this man had clout and credentials.

The second person Paul brought with him was Titus. This is the same Titus that Paul later wrote the book of Titus to, the same one he left in Crete with the authority to "set things in order." Both of these men were vital to the ministry of Paul, but there was one essential difference: Titus was not of Jewish birth. And that was going to be an issue later on when they got to Jerusalem.

Galatians 2:2 *And I went up by revelation, and communicated unto them that gospel which I preach among the Gentiles, but privately to them which were of reputation, lest by any means I should run, or had run, in vain.*

There was a reason that Paul went to Jerusalem at this time. From this verse, we know that God revealed to him that he should go, and from Acts 15, we know what it was about:

Acts 15:1 *And certain men which came down from Judaea taught the brethren, and said, Except ye be circumcised after the manner of Moses, ye cannot be saved.* **2** *When therefore Paul and Barnabas had no small dissension and disputation with them, they determined that Paul and Barnabas, and certain other of them, should go up to Jerusalem unto the apostles and elders about this question.* **3** *And being brought on their way by the church, they passed through Phenice and Samaria, declaring the conversion of the Gentiles: and they caused great joy unto all the brethren.* **4** *And when they were come to Jerusalem, they were received of the church, and of the apostles and elders, and they declared all things that God had done with them.*

This trip from Antioch to Jerusalem was to settle an issue in the mind of man that was already settled in the mind of God and in the mind of Paul; were works necessary for salvation, especially the Jewish favorite work of circumcision? Paul knew that works had nothing to do with salvation, yet he also knew the importance and influence of the local church, especially the church at Jerusalem. So he went to Jerusalem for a showdown on the issue.

This showdown, this "argument," if you will, was absolutely necessary. I will write more about that shortly, but right now, I want to look at how Paul did it and why because there is something very valuable to learn from his methodology. Notice that when Paul went to Jerusalem for this showdown, he did not call a big meeting, round everybody up, and start pointing fingers. Verse two says that he did this "privately to them which were of reputation." He did it this way so that this trip to Jerusalem would not be "run in vain." In other words, if he had not handled this right, the end result could have been a disaster.

Even though Paul was already arguably the best apostle and most powerful preacher since Christ Himself, he came to Jerusalem in quietness and humility, pulled the apostles aside privately, and explained everything to them.

Please, let this sink in; it is very easy for us, knowing that we are right on the issues, to blow up, cause a scene, and hurt good men who are on the same side we are! Christians in general, and preachers in particular, seem to be pretty bad about this.

Some years back, there was a huge blow-up between four preachers. Two of them did not know it was coming. A younger preacher stormed in, confronted two old men of God that have been serving the Lord longer than he has been alive, and started screaming at them. All of the secretaries in the office heard the screaming. Then the younger preacher's pastor was brought in, and the screaming only got worse. All of that caused a break in fellowship that will probably never be repaired. Every one of those four men is a Bible-believing man. They are all on the same side. Yet they are now bitter enemies, and it was not necessary. There is one thing that could have made things turn out very differently: if that young man had gone in like Paul and Barnabas, quietly and carefully and humbly, then even if they could not come to an agreement on the issue at hand, at least they could have left on good terms, parted ways without hurting each other, and perhaps reconciled later.

Ladies and gentlemen, get in the habit of behaving like Paul when there is a potentially explosive issue! I do not think it is an exaggeration to say that the careful way Paul handled this kept the devil from ruining the work of the church for decades or maybe even centuries.

A Stand for Freedom

Galatians 2:3 *But neither Titus, who was with me, being a Greek, was compelled to be circumcised:* **4** *And that because of false brethren unawares brought in, who came in privily to spy out our liberty which we have in Christ Jesus, that they might bring us into bondage:* **5** *To whom we gave place by subjection, no, not for an hour; that the truth of the gospel might continue with you.*

These three verses tell us what happened when Paul, Titus, and Barnabas got to Jerusalem. Remember me saying that the fact that Titus was a Gentile was going to come into play? When they got there, the issue of circumcision naturally came up, and here was Paul with Titus, a Gentile who obviously would be uncircumcised. Talk about a battleground! There were people there who realized that and immediately made a huge issue of it:

"This is exactly what we have been saying! Paul is going to turn us all into heathens instead of making the heathens like us! We demand that Titus be circumcised and that you tell all the Gentiles that if they want to be saved, they have to be circumcised too!"

Do you remember how careful Paul was in how he approached people who were on his side, the apostles, those great men of God? When it came to the enemies of God, though,

47

people who were teaching a false means of salvation, outright heresy, Paul was not nearly as nice. In verse four, he called them "false brethren." In other words, he said that they were not even saved! He labeled them as people who had somehow crept in, posing as believers, when they were as lost as the devil himself. It is interesting to note that from the very first generation of local churches, the devil has been active in infiltrating them with his own people.

Some people will doubtless think, "How dare Paul judge somebody like that! You can't know a man's heart."

Don't be so sure. In fact, there are cases in which you can know a man's heart, and this is one of them. When someone is teaching a false means of salvation, they either do not know the real way to be saved, or they know the real way and are intentionally teaching error, or both. Either way, that is clearly a person who is not saved!

Paul went on in verse four to call them a bunch of spies who were trying to bring people into bondage. He was accusing them of intentionally trying to deceive people and get control of them.

With people like that, enemies of Christ, you take the exact opposite approach of how you deal with brethren. Paul was humble and careful with the apostles. But when it came to these workers of evil, Paul said, *"We gave place by subjection, no, not for an hour."* In other words, Paul did not even give them a polite nod; he did not let them be heard and then calmly reason against them, he blew them out of the water, and he did so forcefully so that, according to the end of the verse, *"the truth of the gospel might continue with you."*

If we do not confront errors concerning salvation, eventually, people will not even know the real gospel when they hear it. Furthermore, think of the damage this would have done to Titus if Paul had meekly given in on this. Titus trusted Christ and Paul; his confidence in both would have been wrecked had he been handed over to these wolves.

Standing against people when they teach error often seems so mean, so "uncharitable," as the favorite new catchphrase goes. But you would not be "nice and charitable" to someone who tried to kidnap your children or to someone who tried to rape your wife, so why would you be kind and charitable to someone trying to send your wife or children to hell for eternity? Why would you be nice and charitable to those who are trying to wreck and ruin future leaders of the church, such as Titus?

A Solidifying of the Truth

Galatians 2:6 *But of these who seemed to be somewhat, (whatsoever they were, it maketh no matter to me: God accepteth no man's person:) for they who seemed to be somewhat in conference added nothing to me:*

From this verse all the way through verse ten, the enemies of Christ are not mentioned at all. All of these verses refer to the apostles that Paul met with at Jerusalem.

In verse six, Paul is driving two points home that he really wanted the Galatians to know. The first thing he was saying is that when he met in conference with these important men, the ones who "seemed to be somewhat," they agreed with him. They did not add anything to the simple gospel of grace. They did not tell Paul he needed to add works to the blood; they did not demand that he add circumcision to faith; they did not agree with the Judaizers that we needed to be placing ourselves back under the bondage of the law.

To the Galatians, this was important! It really meant something to them to know that the apostles in Jerusalem had already uttered an opinion on the trouble that they were now facing.

But the second thing Paul wanted them to know is found in the parenthesis of verse six. After speaking of those who *"seemed to be somewhat,"* he said, *"whatsoever they were, it maketh no matter to me: God accepteth no man's person."* In other words, Paul was trying to tell them that even though he was glad the apostles agreed with him, even though the Galatians should be glad the apostles agreed with him, it really would not have mattered so much as an ounce if they all disagreed! If Peter, James, and John had all decided that Paul was wrong and the Judaizers were right, Paul was going to keep on preaching the truth because the truth was not dependent on those important men.

This is something we really need to understand. It is nice to have big-name "important preachers" holding forth with us in the truth. But we do not need to be guilty of allegiance to the middleman. Our allegiance goes directly to Christ and the Bible without having to make its way through a man! If tomorrow every preacher we have ever had confidence in all decides to go contrary to Scripture on anything, then it is our duty to continue to follow the Bible even though they have stopped. For 2,000 years, from continent to continent, country to country, age to age, language to language, people have been believing the same things and behaving the same way. We can trace our belief system all the way back to Christ and the apostles for one simple reason—our forefathers did not really care what men said; they only cared what the Bible said.

That is the attitude Paul was expressing here. Thank God for men that God Himself elevates to prominence, but we are not subservient to any of them. No prominent, famous preacher is any more authoritative than an old, unknown, Bible-believing, mountain preacher in the hills of West Virginia that no one has ever heard of. There is no "hierarchy of authority" in Christian doctrine. Our doctrine is decided by the Bible, not by any man.

Galatians 2:7 *But contrariwise, when they saw that the gospel of the uncircumcision was committed unto me, as the gospel of the circumcision was unto Peter;*

"*But contrariwise*" takes us back to the last phrase of verse six. When you put them together, you get this idea: "They did not add one thing to what I was preaching, but on the contrary..."

The thought in verse seven does not stop there, as you can see by the semi-colon, but we are going to let it hang just for a moment and look at this verse before we move on. Paul said here that the gospel of the uncircumcision was committed to him, and the gospel of the circumcision was committed to Peter.

Let me clear one thing up immediately. Paul was not saying that there were two different gospels. He was emphasizing the fact that there was one gospel that was going to two very different groups of people. Those two different groups of people believed and were saved in the exact same way. But on a matter not at all related to salvation, they were behaving differently. The Jews were used to circumcision; it had been in their heritage for thousands of years. The Gentiles were not used to circumcision; it was utterly foreign to them. The Jews that were getting saved were already circumcised and continued to have their children circumcised. The Gentiles that were getting saved were not circumcised and were not having their children circumcised. And it did not make a hill of beans worth of difference! As long as it is not done as an attempt to earn salvation, there was nothing spiritually wrong then with being circumcised or having your kids circumcised, nor is there today. There was also nothing spiritually wrong then with not being circumcised or not having your kids circumcised, nor is there today. Circumcision has no effect on salvation either way. No work at all has anything to do with salvation.

One gospel going to two very different groups of people, two different groups of people believing and being saved in the exact same way. But on a matter not at all related to salvation, they were behaving differently, and there was no problem with it for anyone who truly understood the Bible.

Galatians 2:8 *(For he that wrought effectually in Peter to the apostleship of the circumcision, the same was mighty in me toward the Gentiles:)*

Even though they would never admit it, do you know what most people do not like about God? He will not fit into any of the boxes they keep building for Him. God fits very nicely in His book, but not in our box! Paul reminded the Galatians that it was God that had sent Peter to the stubborn, circumcised Jews and saved bunches of them. And then it was that very same God that sent Paul to the wild, uncircumcised Gentiles and saved even more of them.

Now please stop and think about this: how similar do you think their churches were? Don't you imagine that if you walked into a church full of Jews in those days, and then a week later walked into a church full of Gentiles, even though the doctrine was the same, the book was the same, the blood was the same, that those churches would still be very different?

I am blessed to get to go and preach in a lot of different Bible-believing churches every year, and I have learned something: they are not at all alike! The blood is the same, the book is the same, and the blessed hope is the same, but the churches are not the same.

I preach in one church where the pastor makes all the special singers sing from the back of the church so that no one will see them, and they will not get too proud. I preach in another one where instead of passing the plates, there is a box on the wall, and everyone makes sure no one is watching them when they put something in. In one church, there is one little keyboard, nothing else, and it is played organ style. In another, there will be fifteen men lined up around the walls, all picking guitars! Another church I go to has one of the most organized visitation programs you have ever seen, and they do a good job with it. In another, there is no organized visitation whatsoever, but every week members go to their friends and families and co-workers and tell about what Jesus has done for them, and people get saved by the hundreds each year!

God puts different ministries led by different men into different places, and only the truly arrogant or truly dumb expect them to be "exactly like me" in every regard. The book is the same and the blood is the same, but Peter and Paul were different, and the ministries they started were different as well. Here is a good way to summarize it, and it will help you for the rest of your life if you memorize it:

Uniformity in precepts, liberty in preferences.

Galatians 2:9 *And when James, Cephas, and John, who seemed to be pillars, perceived the grace that was given unto me, they gave to me and Barnabas the right hands of fellowship; that we should go unto the heathen, and they unto the circumcision.*

What a godly, Christ-like attitude! The apostles, these noteworthy men, looked at a man who believed like they did but whose ministry was very different because it was to very different people, and they gave him the right hand of fellowship. They said, in effect, "Paul, it is obvious that we are preaching the exact same gospel. The only things we differ on are the non-essentials. We can live with that. Praise God, go on about your business; we are behind you one hundred percent."

I have a question: why does that attitude seem to be extinct in our day? Holiness today is often determined by how many people you can claim in your "enemies column." I actually heard a man say, with a straight face, "I want to be so separated that John the Baptist couldn't get along with me."

My, my, how "holy."

I can think of several churches that, truth be told, irritate me like scratching fingernails on a blackboard. But as I examine their doctrine, I find that they are not my enemies. It is not their doctrine that bugs me so badly; it is all of their annoying preferences. I am not planning on having them over for a barbeque any time soon, but I am not putting them on my "enemy list" either.

Galatians 2:10 *Only they would that we should remember the poor; the same which I also was forward to do.*

This verse is often looked at as an afterthought, something that does not go with what came before it. But that is not true at all. This verse ties into what came before it in an essential way.

It was not the Gentile churches that were "poor" in this verse. The center of persecution, and therefore the center of poverty among Christians, was in Jerusalem. The apostles were telling Paul, among other things, to have the Gentile believers be mindful of and help with the suffering that the Jewish believers were going through, and Paul was already doing that. Why was that so important? Remember that there were two very different groups of people being saved by the same gospel but behaving very differently in the non-essentials. The only thing that was tying them together was doctrine.

That is fine; it sort of works, but it is also very cold. John put it this way:

1 John 4:7 *Beloved, let us love one another: for love is of God; and every one that loveth is born of God, and knoweth God.*

Jesus put it this way:

John 13:34 *A new commandment I give unto you, That ye love one another; as I have loved you, that ye also love one another.*

This command is mentioned dozens of times in the New Testament in one form or another. Truthfully, the reason that churches that do not preach the truth often gain more people than those that do is that one has truth, but the other has love. Which do you think people will be more likely to gravitate toward?

If a woman is being courted by two men, one of which sends her flowers and the other of which gives her a thesaurus, which one do you think she will choose? She will choose the flower giver and will be irritated, perturbed, annoyed, upset, galled, and chafed at the thesaurus sender.

So you have the truth, but do you have love? Even for people whose preferences on the non-essentials are different from yours? Again, uniformity in precepts, liberty in preferences! Paul came focused on the truth, the apostles wrapped up the conversation focused on love, and both would be necessary for the gospel to be as effective as possible.

Chapter Five
Nose to Nose

Galatians 2:11 *But when Peter was come to Antioch, I withstood him to the face, because he was to be blamed. **12** For before that certain came from James, he did eat with the Gentiles: but when they were come, he withdrew and separated himself, fearing them which were of the circumcision. **13** And the other Jews dissembled likewise with him; insomuch that Barnabas also was carried away with their dissimulation. **14** But when I saw that they walked not uprightly according to the truth of the gospel, I said unto Peter before them all, If thou, being a Jew, livest after the manner of Gentiles, and not as do the Jews, why compellest thou the Gentiles to live as do the Jews? **15** We who are Jews by nature, and not sinners of the Gentiles, **16** Knowing that a man is not justified by the works of the law, but by the faith of Jesus Christ, even we have believed in Jesus Christ, that we might be justified by the faith of Christ, and not by the works of the law: for by the works of the law shall no flesh be justified. **17** But if, while we seek to be justified by Christ, we ourselves also are found sinners, is therefore Christ the minister of sin? God forbid. **18** For if I build again the things which I destroyed, I make myself a transgressor. **19** For I through the law am dead to the law, that I might live unto God. **20** I am crucified with Christ: nevertheless I live; yet not I, but Christ* *liveth in me: and the life which I now live in the flesh I live by the faith of the Son of God, who loved me, and gave himself for me. 21 I do not frustrate the grace of God: for if righteousness come by the law, then Christ is dead in vain.*

Let me give you a scenario and then tell you what is about to happen. Two very angry-looking men are touching noses and not blinking. They are about to fight! Be it physically or with words, they are about to go at it. This happens before every boxing match, and it is where we get the term "going nose to nose." Galatians 2:11-21 gives us the account of the time when Paul and Peter, those great men of God, went nose to nose over a spiritual issue.

A Racial Problem

Galatians 2:11 *But when Peter was come to Antioch, I withstood him to the face, because he was to be blamed.*

Before we even get into the issue that Peter and Paul were at odds over, let's just examine the implications of the fact that they were at odds to begin with. As you examine them both Biblically and historically, you find first of all that Peter was older than Paul. Right after the resurrection, Jesus let us know that Peter was no longer a young man:

John 21:18 *Verily, verily, I say unto thee, **When thou wast young**, thou girdedst thyself, and walkedst whither thou wouldest: but when thou shalt be old, thou shalt stretch forth thy hands, and another shall gird thee, and carry thee whither thou wouldest not.*

But after that, we find that Paul, Saul, was still young:

Acts 7:58 *And cast him out of the city, and stoned him: and the witnesses laid down their clothes at a **young man's** feet, whose name was Saul.*

From these two verses, it is evident that Peter was many years older than Paul. Yet that did not stop Paul from confronting and correcting Peter when he was wrong. And he did so with passion and force. When we read that Paul "withstood him to the face," it means exactly what it sounds like. Paul literally got up in his face over this issue.

With age comes many things, some good, some bad. One of the bad things that comes with it is the feeling that we are never wrong and that it is an insult for a younger person to correct us. Paul apparently did not believe this way, and incidentally, neither did Peter. Look at what Peter wrote about Paul after this:

2 Peter 3:15 *And account that the longsuffering of our Lord is salvation; even as our beloved brother Paul also according to the wisdom given unto him hath written unto you;*

Peter got many things wrong, but praise God, he got this one right. When you are wrong, you are wrong, even when it is a younger person that shows you! Yes, there should be a certain amount of respect and deference given to those who have gotten older, but that does not mean that a younger person cannot or should not correct an older one who is wrong, as long as it is done in the proper place and in the proper time and in the proper manner.

The second thing to notice about this is that Peter had been in the ministry longer than Paul, but again, Paul still corrected him. Again, there should be a certain amount of deference given to those who are seniors in the ministry. But the fact that you have been in the ministry a long time does not make you right about anything and does not mean you should not be corrected. Benny Hinn and Oral Roberts have been in the ministry for a long time. Joyce Myers has been in the ministry for a long time. Get the point?

Galatians 2:12 *For before that certain came from James, he did eat with the Gentiles: but when they were come, he withdrew and separated himself, fearing them which were of the circumcision.*

We do not know exactly when, but at some point, after Paul had gone into Jerusalem, Peter came from Jerusalem to Antioch for a visit to see the churches there. When he came, he at first did exactly right. He sat down with his Gentile brothers in Christ and had meals and fellowship together with them. But sometime shortly after, while he was still there, some folks who were near to James in Jerusalem came by Antioch as well. When they showed up, Peter pulled away and would not even so much as eat with the Gentile Christians anymore.

There are several things we need to see here. First of all, please notice that it does not anywhere say that James demanded this. In fact, it was James who, in verse nine, Paul credited with doing right in this matter and giving Paul the right hand of fellowship to keep doing what he was doing!

Here is what was going on. The church in Jerusalem was still made up primarily of Jews. Even after getting saved, many of them were still observing Jewish customs and habits. That would include things like not eating with Gentiles. It was not right, but old habits die hard. These close-to-James folks who came by were just like that. And Peter, seeing them, was intimidated. Notice that the verse says he "feared those which were of the circumcision." What Peter did here, he did out of fear!

That amazes and disappoints me. Peter was, his entire ministry, like the stock market. Up and down, volatile, unpredictable. When he was right, he was very right: walking on water, "thou are the Christ," preaching on Pentecost.

But when he was wrong, he was very wrong: sinking after walking on the water, "Not so, Lord," denying Jesus.

If there is something we should strive hard for, it is consistency in the right!

Galatians 2:13 *And the other Jews dissembled likewise with him; insomuch that Barnabas also was carried away with their dissimulation.*

Those words *dissembled* and *dissimulation* are great Old English words that mean "to act hypocritically." We will learn more about that as we look at the next verse. For now, just understand that Peter was acting like a hypocrite, other Jews joined him, and it got so bad that even faithful old Barnabas got swept up in it!

There are two things to really grasp here. Number one, your race means less than nothing to God. Number two, when people who are of reputation do wrong, others will follow!

A Revealing Point

Galatians 2:14 *But when I saw that they walked not uprightly according to the truth of the gospel, I said unto Peter before them all, If thou, being a Jew, livest after the manner of Gentiles, and not as do the Jews, why compellest thou the Gentiles to live as do the Jews?*

Paul was not one to back down when people he loved were being hurt. Peter was not doing right, so Paul, in front of all of them, called him on it. But why did he do it this way instead of privately, like we saw him do in the first part of the chapter? Simply because this error had gone public, many people were doing wrong because of the actions of one, and so the only way to stop it was to deal with this one publicly. Here is how Paul formalized that concept to Timothy:

1 Timothy 5:20 *Them that sin rebuke before all, that others also may fear.*

Paul, in front of all of them, spelled out the hypocrisy of Peter. Peter was living like a Gentile and demanding that the Gentiles live like Jews! Peter was not strictly observing the Jewish ceremonial law any longer. He had eaten meals with Gentiles. But now, all of a sudden, he decides that the Gentiles better live like he was not living anymore. What a revealing point! Leaders, never preach or teach that people should live better than you are living. Just live right, teach right, and be consistent enough to be safely followed.

A Right Pathway

Galatians 2:15 *We who are Jews by nature, and not sinners of the Gentiles,* **16** *Knowing that a man is not justified by the works of the law, but by the faith of Jesus Christ, even we have believed in Jesus Christ, that we might be justified by the faith of Christ, and not by the works of the law: for by the works of the law shall no flesh be justified.*

Paul reminded Peter that they were Jews by nature, not sinners of the Gentiles. In other words, they had a long spiritual heritage and had possessed the Scriptures for generations. If anyone should have been able to be justified by "being Jewish," they should have. And yet, both of them knew that had never happened and could never happen. Paul especially understood ultra-clearly what it took to get from point A to point B. If point A is being a sinner, and point B is getting saved, there is only one line that connects them, and it is a straight, red line drawn in blood, sealed by grace. Jews were getting saved by this plan, God's plan, and now Peter was sending the message that that plan would not work! If what Peter was now doing and saying was correct, Jesus may as well not have come and died, Calvary may as well not have happened, and if it did, the tomb may as well still be occupied. They just could not get over the law, but as the end of verse four says, *"By the works of the law shall no flesh be justified."*

You can become a lot of things by the works of the flesh (proud, religious, moral, clean-cut, respectable), but the one thing you can never become is the only thing that will get you into heaven: justified!

A Righteous Paradox

Galatians 2:17 *But if, while we seek to be justified by Christ, we ourselves also are found sinners, is therefore Christ the minister of sin? God forbid.*

The type of writing that you see from here to the end of the chapter, a paradox in every thought, is something that Paul did a lot of and was very good at. Romans is loaded with it. In this verse, Paul poses this thought: if we seek to be justified by Christ, yet also seek to be justified by the law, we have to know that the law always points out the fact that we are guilty. Christ justifies, the law condemns. So does the ministry of Christ bring us into sin? God forbid, let it never be under any circumstances! (Henry, 656)

Galatians 2:18 *For if I build again the things which I destroyed, I make myself a transgressor.*

Paul, through the inspiration of the Holy Ghost, destroyed the idea that the law was necessary to be justified. He killed it. If he revived it, like Peter was doing, he would be condemning himself all over again. If you are in prison, and someone tears it down block by block for you, you are free. But if you then turn around and rebuild it around you, you are imprisoned again, and it is your own fault. And by turning back to the law for righteousness in front of those Gentiles, that is what Peter was doing, and that is what he was teaching them to do.

Galatians 2:19 *For I through the law am dead to the law, that I might live unto God.*

Paul was under the law as heavily as a man could be. He found out that there was no hope in the law. Staring the law squarely in the face, the law killed any hope that Paul had in it. He died to it, which finally allowed him to live when he met Christ. And that brings us to one of the most wonderful verses in all of the Bible:

Galatians 2:20 *I am crucified with Christ: nevertheless I live; yet not I, but Christ liveth in me: and the life which I now live in the flesh I live by the faith of the Son of God, who loved me, and gave himself for me.*

Paul said, "*I am crucified with Christ.*" Paul had tried his hardest to earn heaven by his works. Finally, he realized that was impossible. The only way he could get to heaven was for the old, sinful him to die and for him to somehow live again after that as a totally new, perfect man. So Christ went to the cross and died, but not for Himself; He died for Paul, and me, and you, and everyone. So truthfully, Paul was crucified with Christ, as I was, and as you were. But it did not stop there. Paul went on to say that even though he had been crucified with Christ, "*nevertheless I live;*" Just as Christ had died and then risen again, when the old sinner that Paul was died, Paul was re-born as a child of God, a new creature in Christ, with all of the righteousness of Christ imputed to his account, making him perfect in God's sight. If we are saved, the sinner that we once were has died forever and can never come back to life. That is one way we know we are eternally secure!

Next, he said, "*Yet not I, but Christ liveth in me.*" Before Paul got saved, everything he did was empowered by Paul himself. He was "sufficient" for what he was doing. Anyone can be sufficient enough to be a sinner and live like a sinner. But once he got saved, everything he did became empowered by Christ, who lived in him through the Holy Spirit. You can live a sinful life under your own power, but you cannot live a Christian life under your own power. This is why so many people get frustrated. They try to live right without ever having been saved, and it just does not work. Once a person finally gets saved, Christ living in them produces the Christian life.

Next came, "*And the life I now live in the flesh I live by the faith of the Son of God.*" Before he got saved, he lived by sight. After he got saved, Paul learned to live by faith:

2 Corinthians 5:7 (*For we walk by faith, not by sight:*)

When a person gets saved, they learn this. Before salvation, it is all about seeing everything ahead of time, like a giant floodlight is lighting the way. After you get saved, it is about reaching for the hand of Christ and letting Him lead you through every dark valley, holding His hand, and hearing His voice.

Lastly, Paul said that the Son of God was the One who *"loved me, and gave Himself for me."* It was not the fact that Christ died that finally won Paul's heart; it was the fact that Christ died *for him* that won Paul's heart. It is not just that God is love, in general, it is that God loves you and me, specifically.

Galatians 2:21 *I do not frustrate* [thwart the effect of] *the grace of God: for if righteousness come by the law, then Christ is dead in vain.*

This summarizes the entire argument. It can be by your efforts in your life or by Christ's effort on Calvary, but not by both. If you try to add works to salvation, you are thwarting the effect of the grace of God, and thwarted grace will not save you. If you dilute grace at all, if you water it down with any amount of works, it will not save you. All it will do is enslave you in a yoke of bondage.

Chapter Six
Oh Foolish (Fill in the Blank)

Galatians 3:1 *O foolish Galatians, who hath bewitched you, that ye should not obey the truth, before whose eyes Jesus Christ hath been evidently set forth, crucified among you?* **2** *This only would I learn of you, Received ye the Spirit by the works of the law, or by the hearing of faith?* **3** *Are ye so foolish? having begun in the Spirit, are ye now made perfect by the flesh?* **4** *Have ye suffered so many things in vain? if it be yet in vain.* **5** *He therefore that ministereth to you the Spirit, and worketh miracles among you, doeth he it by the works of the law, or by the hearing of faith?* **6** *Even as Abraham believed God, and it was accounted to him for righteousness.* **7** *Know ye therefore that they which are of faith, the same are the children of Abraham.* **8** *And the scripture, foreseeing that God would justify the heathen through faith, preached before the gospel unto Abraham, saying, In thee shall all nations be blessed.* **9** *So then they which be of faith are blessed with faithful Abraham.* **10** *For as many as are of the works of the law are under the curse: for it is written, Cursed is every one that continueth not in all things which are written in the book of the law to do them.* **11** *But that no man is justified by the law in the sight of God, it is evident: for, The just shall live by faith.* **12** *And the law is not of faith: but, The man that doeth them shall live in them.* **13** *Christ hath redeemed us from the* *curse of the law, being made a curse for us: for it is written, Cursed is every one that hangeth on a tree:* **14** *That the blessing of Abraham might come on the Gentiles through Jesus Christ; that we might receive the promise of the Spirit through faith.*

There are some things in life that are just dumb, dumb, dumb...

In Knox County, Tennessee, a man was in court on charges of auto theft. As he stood before the judge, the judge said to him, "How do you plead?" Instead of answering, "Not guilty," the man instead said, "Well, before we go any further, judge, let me explain why I stole the car..." Shortest trial in history. (Butler, 17)

Detective Chris Stewart, an officer in Georgia, tells of the time that he went to investigate a purse snatching. A woman in a shopping complex had had her purse stolen, and she gave him a description of the suspect. A short time later, he and his partner spotted a man that looked like what the woman had described. So they picked him up, told him a woman's purse had been snatched, and that they were going to take him back to the scene for a positive identification. When they got there, before anyone could speak, Mr. Genius criminal said, "Yeah, that's her, officer, she's the woman I robbed..." (Butler, 19)

Sheer genius.

But far more foolish people can be found every day working, saving, living decent, respectable lives. How are they more foolish? By knowing about grace, knowing about the blood of Jesus, and still being suckered into believing in some form of a works-based salvation or a tradition-based holiness. And that is what happened to the Galatians.

A Bewitching

Galatians 3:1 *O foolish Galatians, who hath bewitched you, that ye should not obey the truth, before whose eyes Jesus Christ hath been evidently set forth, crucified among you?*

68

What a way to begin a chapter, those first three words! O foolish Galatians... That has to cut! Yet the same thing that was true of them is true of so many others. Based on the exact problem Paul was dealing with, it could fairly read O foolish Catholics, or O foolish Church of Christ, or O foolish Mormons, or O foolish Jehovah's Witnesses, or O foolish Seventh Day Adventists, or O foolish Muslims, or O foolish Christian Scientists, or O foolish Scientologists, or O foolish Buddhists, or O foolish Hindus, or on and on and on! It may not be popular to say, but it is true: anyone or any group who tries to find salvation in works is foolish!

Paul said, "*O foolish Galatians, who hath bewitched you.*" That is a picturesque word, and it means what it sounds like. "Who has cast some sort of spell over you? Who has allured and enticed you like the witch did Hansel and Gretel? What gingerbread house are they offering in order to get you to give up your freedom?"

O foolish Galatians, who hath bewitched you, that ye should not obey the truth.

There is truth, and there are lies. The truth is that salvation cannot come by works, and everything else is a lie! To add works to faith when you should know better is literally an act of disobedience, not just a matter of being misinformed. They should have known this because according to the last part of this verse:

...before whose eyes Jesus Christ hath been evidently set forth, crucified among you?

That phrase means that by Paul and others, they had been made to know very clearly the crucifixion of Christ and what it meant. Knowing of the sacrifice He made, there was no way they should have fallen for the lies of the Judaizers.

Galatians 3:2 *This only would I learn of you, Received ye the Spirit by the works of the law, or by the hearing of faith?*

That is what you call a very good question. These Christians in Galatia had received the Spirit of God by placing their faith in Jesus Christ, not by circumcision, or the Sabbath, or any other work. The law did nothing for them; faith did everything. That being the case, why would they want to go running to the law?

As a pastor, I see this so often. A person will come and get saved, Christ rescues them from a life of sin, and then suddenly, so-called Christians who have never even tried to win them to God show up, telling them why the church that won them to Christ is wrong and how they need to do some work or another to really be right. The most common one I encounter with frightening regularity is when we win someone to Christ, and the very next week, when that person goes to work and tells everyone what happened, someone of the Pentecostal persuasion, who never witnessed to them at all, tells them they need to come to their church and learn to speak in tongues and receive some second blessing/second filling. On more than one occasion, those people have actually said, "The Baptists are good for winning people to the Lord, but if you really want to have the Holy Spirit and all of His gifts, you need to come to a Pentecostal church."

It is Judaizing repackaged for the modern age.

Galatians 3:3 *Are ye so foolish? having begun in the Spirit, are ye now made perfect by the flesh?*

Once again Paul used the word *foolish*. He was serious about their stupidity! And in this case, their stupidity was that they believed they could be saved by grace, but they could only be "made perfect" by the works of the flesh. May I translate that for you, please? This was the part about Judaizing that said, "Well, maybe you can get initial salvation by grace, but you can only get final salvation by works." I was sent a seven-hundred-page book espousing that nonsense. But it was nonsense, it is nonsense, and it will always be nonsense. First of all, the Bible

70

never mentions or even hints at the idea that salvation is divided between "initial salvation" and "final salvation." When you get saved, that very moment, before you can do a single good work, you become a new creature in Christ (2 Corinthians 5:17) and are sealed unto the day of redemption (Ephesians 4:30) and can never perish (John 5:24). All of that does not happen weeks or months after you get saved after you have managed by your efforts to make yourself acceptable to God. It happens at the very moment that you place your faith in Jesus Christ as your Savior. Do not ever let anyone tell you that you get saved by grace but stay saved by works. Anyone that believes that is a foolish fill-in-the-blank.

And that also demonstrates a bit about what I have been alluding to since the first chapter, that this was a two-pronged attack, an attack both on salvation and sanctification. You see, if you have to do works after salvation to achieve final salvation, then you are earning holiness by the works you do and therefore cannot be holy without those works. It is bondage on both sides of the coin.

Galatians 3:4 *Have ye suffered so many things in vain? if it be yet in vain.*

When the Galatians got saved, they started getting persecuted. As Barnes put it, "They were not those connected with the observance of the Jewish rites. They had suffered on account of their having embraced the gospel – the system of justification by a crucified Redeemer; and now, if those sentiments were wrong, why their sufferings had been wholly in vain." (Lindner)

Simply put, it was not on account of their keeping the Jewish law that they got persecuted; it was on account of their accepting Christ. And now some Judaizers were saying, "Hey! If you will just convert to Judaism along with that grace, you will be in something recognizable to the state, and you can quit being persecuted!" So Paul was saying, "Are you really going to

71

throw in the towel so easily? What about those of you who have been killed for the faith? Are you going to make their deaths be in vain, meaning nothing? Some of you have been tortured; others have had family members taken from you. Are you going to make all of that be in vain, counting for nothing? No. You were told the truth, you believed the truth, you suffered for the truth, keep living in the truth instead of under a spell!"

That "if" that Paul uttered at the end of that verse was a window into his heart. He was unsure of them. He was saying, "I really hope this is not the case; please tell me I am wrong about you, and you are not going that way."

A Believing

Galatians 3:5 *He therefore that ministereth to you the Spirit, and worketh miracles among you, doeth he it by the works of the law, or by the hearing of faith?*

At this point in the text, Paul began to call some character witnesses. The first person he mentioned was himself, the one who won them to God. He said in so many words, "I helped you to get saved; I worked miracles among you; I had the goods. So, did I do it by the works of the law or by faith in Christ?"

Paul never did one miracle by the power of the Sabbath. He never won a single soul to Christ by the power of circumcision. When he was a circumcision-preaching, Sabbath-keeping Jew, he won no one and did no miracles. Things did not start happening until he finally gave up on his efforts to earn salvation and simply believed God!

Galatians 3:6 *Even as Abraham believed God, and it was accounted to him for righteousness.*

The second character witness he called in this issue was Abraham.

So often, I love to say that the difference between Christianity and everything else is two letters: everything else says do while Christianity says done. But while studying this verse, I thought of another way to describe it. Salvation must be either by believing or behaving, one or the other. It cannot be both. So notice here that Abraham, the father to the Jews, the idol to the Judaizers, was saved not by behaving but by believing!

Are we opposed to good behavior? If you have ever, by chance, listened to my preaching, you know better. I make enough people mad by preaching on behavior that it should not even be a question. But we behave because we have believed. That behavior is a result of salvation, never a course to salvation, and never a course to keep salvation.

How was Abraham made righteous? He did so many great things; there is no doubt about that. He left his homeland, not knowing where he was going, just because God told him to. He interceded before God over two cities. He offered up his son Isaac. But for all of that, Abraham was justified, saved, made righteous, by placing his trust and faith in God. We read of this in Genesis 15:6:

Genesis 15:6 *And he believed in the LORD; and he counted it to him* [imputed it] *for righteousness.*

"Abraham, how did you get saved? Was it when you raised the knife on Mount Moriah?"

"No, it wasn't that."

"Well, was it when you left it all behind like God asked?"

"No, again. I got saved when I believed God."

"Well, what was it like after that? How did you manage to stay saved? Was it because you lived such an exemplary, perfect life?"

"Stop laughing, Sarah! Ahem. No, that is definitely not the case. I did some horrible things along the way, including lying and handing my wife over to another man. I stayed saved because once I believed God, He made me His own and never let me go, period!"

Understand this. Abraham was justified many years before circumcision and many years before Mount Moriah. The two most significant works in his life were *after* he got saved. And no work that he did after he did get saved kept him saved. His salvation was all of grace, apart from any works. It is so amazing that it worked for Abraham, but even today, people seem to think they know better than he did!

Galatians 3:7 *Know ye therefore that they which are of faith, the same are the children of Abraham.*

In deep Southern vernacular, let me "splain somethin' " If there had been any Judaizers nearby to hear these words come out of Paul's mouth, they would have done their best to kill him on the spot. You talk about "fightin' words!" Let me paraphrase it for you. Paul basically said, "Look, these Jews who have been coming around acting like they are better than you, they have all missed it. You see, they are not really children of Abraham; you are! They are just mimicking the behavior of Abraham (circumcision, etc.). You have adopted the belief of Abraham! They have his genes; you have his God. You are more a child of Abraham than they are!"

To quote a popular football announcer, "Whoa, Nelly!"

Have you noticed that so often, even Gentile Christians seem to think that Orthodox Jews today have something we do not have? Lots of Gentile Christians seem to think that we need to observe Jewish feasts, adopt Jewish behavior, learn the Jewish language (Hebrew), go to the Holy Land, and look at Jewish things. But why? Please don't get me wrong; I like learning about those things. But I already have the most important Jewish thing ever. I have their Messiah, Jesus the Christ! I have the God of Abraham, and therefore I am a child of Abraham. No Jew is any better than me or you in any way, shape, or form.

Galatians 3:8 *And the scripture, foreseeing that God would justify the heathen through faith, preached before the gospel unto Abraham, saying, In thee shall all nations be* *blessed.* **9** *So then they which be of faith are blessed with faithful Abraham.*

There is that word justify again. When considered fully, it means "The Judicial act whereby God declares the believing sinner as righteous based on what Jesus did on Calvary." God came to do this for us, heathens, and He let Jewish Abraham know about it thousands of years ago. This verse is a quote from Genesis 12:3. It lets us know that we who are of faith are blessed with faithful Abraham. Not we who have been circumcised, not we who keep the Sabbath, not we who observe the feast days, not we who try to behave as an Old Testament Jew, but we who are of faith. We who have believed in the God of Abraham now share in the blessings of Abraham.

It is for this reason, among many others, that it makes no sense at all to try and become "more Jewish" as Christians. Salvation must be by belief or behavior, but it cannot be by both. And thank God in heaven, it is very clear that our salvation is by belief. And it is good that that is the case because even on our very best days, our behavior can never be good enough to satisfy the demands of a thrice-holy God.

A Basis

Have you ever wondered what Paul based all of this on? Was it just his experience on the Damascus Road? That truly was an awesome experience! But Paul did not base any of this on any of his experiences. Everything he was saying had one basis: the Bible! Every argument Paul ever made was based on the Bible. These last five verses will demonstrate that because every single one of them is drawn from one or more Old Testament passages.

Galatians 3:10 *For as many as are of the works of the law are under the curse: for it is written, Cursed is every one that continueth not in **all** things which are written in the book of the law to do them.*

75

Here is where Paul got that from.

Deuteronomy 27:26 *Cursed be he that confirmeth not* ***all*** *the words of this law to do them. And all the people shall say, Amen.*

So what is taught here? Simply this: if you are trusting in the works of the law to save you, you are not in Christ; you are under a curse. You cannot possibly keep **all** of the law perfectly. It is impossible. In the history of the world, no one but Christ has ever done it, and no one ever will. But if you are counting on the law to save you, you have gotten yourself into a bad predicament because "almost perfect" is the exact same as "broke every single one." It is **all** or nothing. You do not break *a* law of God; you break THE law of God.

This is what makes it so sad when people get enamored with the Jewish law. Groups such as many of the Messianic Judaism adherents, some Judaistic Adventists, and others believe that you need to keep the Old Testament law to be saved or that keeping the law makes you more right with God, more appropriate of a believer than those who do not. Here is just a bit of what they (Messianic Judaism) believe, in their own words:

"Messianic Jews and Christians both embrace the entire Hebrew Bible and the New Testament as Spirit-inspired Holy Writ. However, many Messianic Jews continue to live by the first five books of the Bible, called the Torah, something most Christians do not do."

"Messianic Jewish people observe the Sabbath, or Shabbat, during the traditional Jewish time starting before sunset on Friday evening until Saturday night. While there are several theories on when the Christian church deviated from the traditional Jewish day of Shabbat, Christians have been observing the Sabbath on Sundays since the second century."

"Most Christians do not observe the biblical commandments regarding dietary practices. These include the avoidance of scavengers of land or sea, with the exception of mammals that both chew the cud and have hooves, like sheep, goats, and deer. For many Messianic Jewish people, the basic biblical commandments found in the Torah are still observed. This observance enables Messianic Jewish people to maintain their God-given identities as Jews." (*Difference Between Messianic Judaism and Christianity* 2017))

So much of this sounds so lofty on the surface. But the problem, among others, is that the law they are trying to keep cannot simply be treated as a buffet bar. Paul made it clear that it is all or nothing. And yet they only keep a small portion of the law! They never sacrifice animals; they wear clothing of mixed fabrics; they live in houses without banisters around the roof; they do not use the bathroom in an open field with a shovel; they do not throw their clothes away if they come into contact with a dead body, I could go on with this list for hours. They cherry-pick certain parts of the law and ignore the other ninety-five percent of it. And at least the ones that I have known personally also look down their noses at us "ignorant heathens." But people who put themselves under the law are putting themselves under a curse, and that isn't smart, no matter how many wonderful websites you produce to promote it.

Mind you, the law still serves some valid purposes. For one, as we will see shortly in the book, it points out our deficiency and thereby takes us straight to Christ for help:

Galatians 3:24 *Wherefore the law was our schoolmaster to bring us unto Christ, that we might be justified by faith.*

Further, all of it serves as a good learning guide:

Romans 15:4 *For whatsoever things were written aforetime were written for our learning, that we through patience and comfort of the scriptures might have hope.*

And much of it was moral in nature rather than civil or ceremonial and either repeated by Christ for today, or at least not set aside by anything that was said or done in the New Testament, and therefore entirely binding for today. So there was and is a good purpose for the law, but salvation was not one of those purposes. And the next verse, one of the most important in the Bible on salvation, will make that abundantly clear.

Galatians 3:11 *But that no man is justified by the law in the sight of God, it is evident: for, The just shall live by faith.*

It is hard to fathom a clearer, more powerful statement than *"But that no man is justified by the law in the sight of God, it is evident* [clear]." Not one person in the entire history of mankind has ever been justified by the works of the law, not a single one. And none ever will.

Notice now that last phrase, *"the just shall live by faith."* That word "just" is short for "justified." And again, this is a quote from the Old Testament:

Habakkuk 2:4 *Behold, his soul which is lifted up is not upright in him: but the just shall live by his faith.*

When it says, *"the just shall live by faith,"* it means, "The ones who are justified are made alive by their faith. They were dead in sins, but when they trusted Christ in simple faith, they came to life in Him." This is one more way Paul could say, "Works of the law will just leave you dead. Only faith in Christ will justify you, save you, make you alive."

This verse means more to you than you may know. Many of you today are physically alive because of this verse. Martin Luther, the former Catholic priest who finally came to saving faith in Christ, made this great verse, with its doctrine of justification by faith, the watchword of the Reformation. (Search Tools)

That event helped to break the stranglehold of the church of Rome. Up until then, people who believed like us were hunted down and killed without a real trial and without mercy. Though Martin Luther was not a Baptist, his salvation has led to some wonderful, fear-free years for us.

Galatians 3:12 *And the law is not of faith: but, The man that doeth them shall live in them.*

Let's look at one of the Old Testament verses this comes from:

Leviticus 18:5 *Ye shall therefore keep my statutes, and my judgments: which if a man do, he shall live in them: I am the LORD.*

So what do these verses mean? How is Paul applying them? Notice that he first of all says, *"The law is not of faith."* That is true of every law system in every country in every age. You do not have to "believe in the law." You do not have to "have faith in the law."

You are driving down the road, obeying the posted speed, staying in your lane, buckled up, hands on the ten and two position when suddenly you are pulled over. The officer gets out and walks over to your vehicle, looks down at you from behind those sunglasses, and says, "License and registration, please." You hand it over, and he walks back to his car. You can see him on his radio, talking to Headquarters. He comes back in a minute and hands you a ticket with a $375.00 fine on it.

You say, "What's this for, officer? I was obeying all of the traffic laws!"

And he says, "You sure were, but here's the thing. You were obeying all the law, but I can tell you do not have any faith in those laws. I can see it just by looking at you. So even though you're obeying the law, I'm giving you a ticket for not really believing in the law."

Has that ever happened to anybody? Of course not! You cannot be charged with "not having faith in a law;" you can only be charged for actually breaking a law! Paul's point is this: faith and the law have absolutely nothing to do with each other. This is just one more thing that makes it so ridiculous when people tell you what you have to do to get saved or what you have to avoid doing to stay saved. Faith and the law have nothing to do with each other.

The last part of that verse, Galatians 3:12, presents us with what we call a "hopeless situation." And that is exactly the way God intended it. *"The man that doeth them* [the works of the law] *shall live in them."* Does this mean that Paul has changed his mind? You only have to ask one question to figure it out: how much of the law would a man have to do to live in them? All of them! So was God, through Paul, trying to give us hope in this or trying to let us see just how hopeless that idea is? Hopeless, absolutely hopeless, which is why the next two verses say what they do:

Galatians 3:13 *Christ hath redeemed us from the curse of the law* [not the "hope" of the law, the curse of the law!], *being made a curse for us: for it is written, Cursed is every one that hangeth on a tree:* **14** *That the blessing of Abraham might come on the Gentiles through Jesus Christ; that we might receive the promise of the Spirit through faith.*

God made the law to show us how hopeless we are, how little our own efforts could do for us. And that is why He also placed this verse in the law, which was just quoted in Galatians 3:13:

Deuteronomy 21:23 *His body shall not remain all night upon the tree, but thou shalt in any wise bury him that day; (for he that is hanged is accursed of God;) that thy land be not defiled, which the LORD thy God giveth thee for an inheritance.*

This type of hanging was not by rope. It was by piercing; it was by being nailed or in some way fastened to a tree. The New Testament word for it is "crucifixion." Robertson said, "The allusion was to exposure of dead bodies on stakes or

crosses (Jos 10:26)… It was used of gallows, crosses, etc."
(Lindner, Robertson)

Jesus had to be crucified in order to place Himself under
the curse of the law so that we could be redeemed from the curse
of the law. That is the only way the blessing of Abraham could
come upon the Gentiles! It is the only way we (heathens) or they
(Jews) could be redeemed from hell. It is the only way we could
receive the promise of the Spirit, meaning His indwelling in our
hearts, and His constant influence in our lives.

I am in favor of good behavior, but you do not get saved,
nor do you stay saved, by your behavior. You get saved by once
and for all time placing your faith, trust, belief in Jesus Christ.
Anyone who says otherwise is just a foolish fill-in-the-blank.

Chapter Seven
Checking Up on Our Inheritance

Galatians 3:15 *Brethren, I speak after the manner of men; Though it be but a man's covenant, yet if it be confirmed, no man disannulleth, or addeth thereto.* **16** *Now to Abraham and his seed were the promises made. He saith not, And to seeds, as of many; but as of one, And to thy seed, which is Christ.* **17** *And this I say, that the covenant, that was confirmed before of God in Christ, the law, which was four hundred and thirty years after, cannot disannul, that it should make the promise of none effect.* **18** *For if the inheritance be of the law, it is no more of promise: but God gave it to Abraham by promise.* **19** *Wherefore then serveth the law? It was added because of transgressions, till the seed should come to whom the promise was made; and it was ordained by angels in the hand of a mediator.* **20** *Now a mediator is not a mediator of one, but God is one.* **21** *Is the law then against the promises of God? God forbid: for if there had been a law given which could have given life, verily righteousness should have been by the law.* **22** *But the scripture hath concluded all under sin, that the promise by faith of Jesus Christ might be given to them that believe.* **23** *But before faith came, we were kept under the law, shut up unto the faith which should afterwards be revealed.* **24** *Wherefore the law was our schoolmaster to bring us unto Christ, that we might be justified* *by faith. 25 But after that faith is come, we are no longer under a schoolmaster. 26 For ye are all the children of God by faith in Christ Jesus. 27 For as many of you as have been baptized into Christ have put on Christ. 28 There is neither Jew nor Greek, there is neither bond nor free, there is neither male nor female: for ye are all one in Christ Jesus. 29 And if ye be Christ's, then are ye Abraham's seed, and heirs according to the promise.*

Being poor and from a poor family has certain advantages. For instance, no one ever argues over the will! In rich families, you often find that a "close-knit family" is not so close-knit after all when there is an inheritance to argue over. But poor folks do not have to worry about that. When all mom or pop has to leave is a stack of bills, I can promise you that everyone is willing to let someone else have it!

Some years back, a man named Baron Hilton decided to change his will. You may never have heard of him, but I bet you have heard of his granddaughter, Paris. Apparently, Mr. Hilton was embarrassed by his granddaughter's behavior. By the way, he was the one with all of the money in the family. He was in his eighties, and the entire family seemed to be licking their chops at the thought of his demise. But Baron Hilton changed his will, leaving most everything to charity! Turns out that poor Paris was not going to be an instant billionaire after all. I am quite certain you, dear reader, are appropriately brokenhearted over that. (Nichols, 2007)

Before that happened, though, I wonder how often she checked up on Grandpop's money to see what she was going to have coming to her. When you know or think that you have a load coming to you, you know you would want to check on it too.

Well, in the spiritual realm, that is actually a good thing. Taking time to remind ourselves about the riches we have in Christ can help to keep us from falling for heretics that come by offering worthless trinkets!

Let's cover this passage by asking a series of questions.

Who is in the will?

When it comes to an inheritance, this is the first thing that everybody wants to know. Did great uncle Edward leave me anything? I know I accidentally fed his Babe Ruth autographed baseball to my dog when I was a kid; I wonder if he ever forgot about that?

The issue that Paul was debating the Judaizers over in the epistle to the Galatians was a question of inheritance. Could the inheritance of God come to heathen Gentiles, or does it only go to the circumcised, orthodox Jews? Did the Gentiles need to become like the Jews in order to get the inheritance? So in this section, Paul starts explaining this issue in light of a last will and testament.

Galatians 3:15 *Brethren, I speak after the manner of men* [In other words, "I am going to use a human illustration to explain this"]*; Though it be but a man's covenant,* [last will and testament] *yet if it be confirmed, no man disannulleth, or addeth thereto.*

This is such a simple yet iron-clad concept. When a family gathers in the lawyer's office, and he breaks out great uncle Edward's will, if that will has been examined and certified to be legal and in order, if it is, in Paul's words, "confirmed," then no one can disannul it or add to it.

The inheritance that God has given us cannot be revoked, changed, lessened, or taken away by the Judaizers or anyone else. Our inheritance is not dependent on man; it is given to us by God.

Galatians 3:16 *Now to Abraham and his seed were the promises made. He saith not, And to seeds, as of many; but as of one, And to thy seed, which is Christ.*

Notice, please, that Paul went back to the Old Testament yet again and made a very important distinction based on one single letter. Quoting Genesis 17:7, Paul said the promise, the inheritance, was not to Abraham's seeds, plural; it was to his seed, singular. In case you wonder whether one single letter can really be that significant, just ask yourself, "Do I want my spouse to have a "mate" or "mates?" One letter makes a huge difference, doesn't it!

Paul said, "God did not leave an inheritance for Abraham's seeds, as to many, but to his seed, to only one, and that one is Christ."

In other words, the real inheritance of Abraham through God does not come to Jews just because they have been circumcised and keep the Sabbath and follow the traditions of the elders. The inheritance of Abraham through God comes to anyone, Jew or Gentile, who receives Christ by faith as Lord and Savior! The Judaizers kept telling the Gentiles that they needed to become proselytes to Judaism to get the inheritance of God. They said, "You need to become of our seed." Paul said, "No, there is only one real seed of Abraham, and it is anyone who has received Christ, Jew or Gentile."

Ladies and Gentlemen, if you have been saved, you are in the will. Whether you are Jew or Gentile, man or woman, black or white, circumcised or not. If you have been born again, you are in the will, and no one can write you out of it!

How strong is the will?

Galatians 3:17 *And this I say, that the covenant, that was confirmed before of God in Christ, the law, which was four hundred and thirty years after, cannot disannul, that it should make the promise of none effect.*

This is one of the most important verses in the entire Bible when it comes to salvation, the law, and works. It introduces an element of time that all by itself should settle the issue. Remember that we are talking about Abraham, about the fact that he was saved by faith, and about the fact that his covenant, his inheritance for us, is by grace instead of by works. When God came to Abraham and confirmed the covenant for him and for us, how many of the ten commandments had been written? None of them! In fact, not a single Mosaic law had yet been given. The promise of Abraham pre-dated the law by 430 years! Four hundred thirty years before anyone ever had a single thought about being saved by keeping the law, God had already promised Abraham that he and his seed would be saved by belief.

God put that in covenant form. He put it as a "last will and testament." No law that came along later can invalidate the will that has already been established for 430 years. The will is so strong, so firmly established that the law could not break it. The Jews kept looking back to Moses for the plan of salvation; they should have been looking back 430 years earlier to Abraham for the plan of salvation.

Before we move on to the next verse, though, we should deal with a chronological question that this verse brings up, namely the period of 430 years. It is mentioned as well back in Exodus:

Exodus 12:40 *Now the sojourning of the children of Israel, who dwelt in Egypt, was four hundred and thirty years.*

Here is the question these passages bring up. It was significantly more than thirty years from the time God gave His promise to Abraham to the time the Children of Israel, beginning with Joseph, went down into Egypt. In fact, it is somewhere around 183 years. So if we add that to 400 years of slavery in Egypt, we end up with way more than 430 years until the giving of the law; we end up with something more like 583 years. And believe me, Bible scoffers love to point out things like this, so you better know what to do with them when they do.

So here is how all of the numbers work because the Bible has no mistakes; we just have flawed minds that often assume some things and miss others. From the time God gave the covenant to the giving of the law was indeed 430 years, just like Galatians and Exodus say. The flaw comes in when people assume that the nation started with Jacob. It did not. The nation of Israel started with Abraham. So the clock starts ticking with Abraham, not Jacob, and certainly not Joseph.

It is in Genesis 12:1-4 that the 430 years begin, when God confirms the covenant with Abraham and tells him of the four hundred years of affliction. And in that very same chapter, and chapter thirteen, we find Abraham right then in Egypt.

The four hundred years begin thirty years later in Genesis 21 when Ishmael, born of Hagar the Egyptian, mocks and persecutes Isaac at his weaning. For the next 163 years, all the while they are in Canaan, they are under Egyptian influence; all of Canaan is. They were doubtless in and out of Egypt constantly, just as Abraham had been. In Genesis 37, Joseph is actually sold into Egypt. Two hundred thirty-seven years later, after the very serious part of the entire nation in bondage as slaves, the Exodus occurs.

So the mistake commonly made is assuming that the four-hundred-year period was four hundred years of national slavery starting after the time of Joseph or even starting with Joseph. But the Bible never says that anywhere. The four hundred years started with the one-on-one persecution of Ishmael of Egyptian descent through his mother, persecuting Isaac of Abraham. And that was thirty years after God confirmed the covenant with Abraham, just like Exodus 12 and Galatians 3 say. (Wright, 2015)

But back to the doctrinal subject at hand, Paul's point was that the Jews kept looking back to Moses for the plan of salvation; they should have been looking back 430 years earlier to Abraham for the plan of salvation!

Galatians 3:18 *For if the inheritance be of the law, it is no more of promise: but God gave it to Abraham by promise.*

From the time of Abraham, the inheritance had been of promise. What promise? The promise that Abraham was saved by believing and that all his future seed would be as well. If what God gave Moses made the inheritance come by law, then God had broken His promise. Could that be? No, because "God gave it to Abraham by promise." God never, ever breaks His promises. How strong is the will? So strong that the very law itself could not and cannot break it! The law was 430 years too late to the party.

But that brings us to another obvious question.

What, then, is the purpose of the law?

If the law was not given until 430 years after the promise of salvation by grace, why did there even need to be a law? Since we now clearly know that salvation is not the purpose of the law, what is its purpose? That, in fact, is exactly what Paul asked:

Galatians 3:19 *Wherefore then serveth the law?*

But he did not just ask the question; he also answered it:

Galatians 3:19 *Wherefore then serveth the law? It was added because of transgressions, till the seed should come to whom the promise was made; and it was ordained by angels in the hand of a mediator.*

The law was added 430 years after the promise for one reason: it was added because of our transgressions. In other words, it was the straight edge to show us how crooked we are! Yes, it obviously helped a society to function; no society can function efficiently or safely without laws. But in the spiritual realm, the law was added because of our transgressions. God wrote out a detailed law so we could see how far off the mark we are. The law is not to make us straight but to show us we are not straight.

Let me illustrate that. In construction, what does a level do?

If you said, "Well, duh, it levels things, everybody knows that!" then I have disappointing news for you: you are dead wrong! A level never "leveled" anything! All a level does is show you how far out of level something is, so you can adjust it accordingly. Many times while building our church buildings, we would put up a metal stud, then lay a level against it. Invariably, the stud was unlevel, leaning one way or the other. Once we figured out which way the stud needed to go, we took a hammer and whacked the stud into place! The level did not level up the stud; the hammer did that. All the level did was show us where the hammer needed to hit.

It is the exact same with the law. The law is a level. It does not "level" us, it shows us how unlevel we are in God's sight.

There is a time period added here as well. Paul said the law *"was added because of transgressions, till the seed should come to whom the promise was made."* That, dear reader, is the Lord Jesus Christ. The law had a time period in which it was to hold sway, and that was from the time of Moses until the time of Christ. That is why, after Christ, Paul was able to say:

Romans 6:14b *...for ye are not under the law, but under grace.*

Breathe! Enjoy the freedom to know that you can just love God and live right without having to worry about whether or not you missed some little piece of the ceremonial law and are now unclean and must therefore wash yourself and remain out of the camp for the next seven days. Life is a lot simpler than that now. Thank God, we are not under the law; we are under grace.

The last part of verse nineteen introduces us to a fact that often goes overlooked. When God gave the law, angels played a part in it. The word "ordained" here means to "set in order." The law that God gave, He allowed the angels to help arrange it. The writer of Hebrews said the same thing:

Hebrews 2:2 *For if the word spoken by angels was stedfast, and every transgression and disobedience received a just recompence of reward;*

The mediator spoken of in verse nineteen was Moses. So God gave the law, allowed angels to help arrange it, and Moses brought it from divinity to humanity. That ought to let you know just how important the law was, even though it has no power at all to save anyone.

Galatians 3:20 *Now a mediator is not a mediator of one, but God is one.*

This verse is designed to tell us a little bit about the God who has promised us our inheritance. Paul just got done telling us about the law and reminding us that Moses was the mediator between God and man on the subject of the law in the sense that God gave the law out to Moses, and Moses then turned around and gave it out to us. Springboarding off of that thought of a mediator, Paul came back to the subject of our inheritance through grace. Just like the law had a mediator, so does grace. "*A mediator is not a mediator of one,*" he is the mediator of two. A mediator goes between two or more parties. But when it comes to grace, God is one. In other words, He plays both the role of the giver and the mediator; we are just the recipient. God the Father gives us grace through the mediating work of God the Son, and we receive it.

The point of all this is that the Galatians did not need the Judaizers, and neither do we! If we were saved by the law, we might need them. After all, give them enough credit to know that they knew the law very, very well. They could quote it line by line and verse by verse and never miss a syllable. But we are not saved by the law, we are saved by grace, and therefore we do not need them! We do not need anybody to "go between God and us so we can be saved," believing in Jesus is simple enough for a child to do it.

91

There are things that are so complicated we have to hire others to do them for us. If you build a new house, the odds are that you will hire an architect to draw your blueprints. But are you going to hire an electrician to come into your home each day and flip on light switches for you as you enter a room? Of course not. Flipping on a light switch is something that is so simple anyone can do it. And anyone with a mind to understand can accept Jesus Christ as Savior; we do not need the law for salvation, and we certainly do not need any modern law-givers.

Galatians 3:21 *Is the law then against the promises of God? God forbid: for if there had been a law given which could have given life, verily righteousness should have been by the law.*

Paul was a very perceptive writer. He knew what questions were going to come up based on what he was writing, and in this case, he asked the question for us. Since the law cannot save us or help to save us, is the law the enemy of salvation by believing in Jesus? God forbid! The fact is, the law has a problem that it cannot get over. The problem with it is that there is no law that can give life. If there was, people could have gotten saved by the law. But in every culture, every age, every situation, there has never been a law that could bring salvation.

The law is good at what it does, showing us our need for salvation, but bad at what it cannot do, which is to bring salvation. The law can no more save a soul than a tape measure can build a house. Both can show you what needs to be done, but neither can actually do what needs to be done.

Galatians 3:22 *But the scripture hath concluded all under sin, that the promise by faith of Jesus Christ might be given to them that believe.*

Once again, Paul takes to the Old Testament Scriptures to prove a New Testament fact: "*the Scripture hath concluded,*" despite the best efforts of man to keep the law, that all are under

92

sin. I can show you that from many Old Testament Scriptures, but let me show you just one:

Isaiah 64:6 *But we are all as an unclean thing, and all our righteousnesses are as filthy rags; and we all do fade as a leaf; and our iniquities, like the wind, have taken us away.*

Notice that "we?" That was Isaiah including himself. If there was ever a good man, it was Isaiah! But even Isaiah concluded that the very best people on their very best days in their most law-abiding condition are still utterly lost! That is the bad news. The good news is found at the end of Galatians 3:22:

...that the promise by faith of Jesus Christ might be given to them that believe.

When you finally despair of getting saved by the law, when you finally realize that you can have the patience of Job and the kindness of Mother Teresa and the good behavior of Mary and still be lost, is there anywhere to turn? Yes! It is then that you can finally turn to what God has been offering the entire time, salvation by putting your faith in Jesus Christ, the same way that Abraham himself became justified when he simply believed God.

Galatians 3:23 *But before faith came, we were kept under the law, shut up unto the faith which should afterwards be revealed.*

When verse twenty-three says, *"before faith came,"* it is not saying that there was no salvation by faith before or during the period of the law. Remember that Abraham was saved by faith 430 years before there was a law. So what this means when it speaks of faith is the New Testament, gospel message of Jesus Christ. The Old Testament saints were saved by faith, but they did not have as clear a view of what they were believing in as we do. They had a general knowledge that God had promised to send a Messiah, and they were looking ahead and placing faith in that Messiah that they knew very little about. We have the blessing and luxury of being able to look back and know Jesus very specifically. So before that kind of faith came, people were kept under the law, and that law was keeping them blinded, locked out of any understanding of the coming gospel.

It was not supposed to do that. That is not what God designed it for. Every part of the law actually pointed to Christ, especially every part of the sacrificial law. But when man got hold of the law, the law became an end unto itself. By the closing days of the Old Testament, the law was worshipped almost as if it were God. Many people did not love God anymore; they loved the law that never loved them back, the law that had been so twisted as to shut up, meaning to close them off from the faith which was going to be revealed in Christ.

That verse can be confusing. But not the next one. The next one is one of the clearest verses in the entire Bible on the purpose of the law.

Galatians 3:24 *Wherefore the law was our schoolmaster to bring us unto Christ, that we might be justified by faith.*

Have you ever had a teacher that was so brash and abrasive that you could not stand but that you had to admit was a very good teacher anyway? I have had quite a few of those. And that describes the purpose of the law. It was a hard, brutal, twenty-four-hour-a-day schoolmaster. It had no compassion, no mercy, and no patience. By the time a person had been under the law for a while, do you know what they often figured out? They did not need any more law; they needed some grace! And that was its purpose the entire time. The law was never designed as an end unto itself; it was designed to take man by the hand and bring him to the understanding that he needed Christ. The purpose of the law was to make us so hopeless standing before God, our sovereign judge, that when Jesus stands up and says, "Father, he cannot possibly make the payment that the law demands, but I already have," we will say, "Glory to God, I need that! Jesus, if you are willing to pay, I am willing to believe because I sure do need some help here."

What is in the will for us?

From here to the end of the chapter, we get the goodies; we get to find out what is in Jesus' last will and testament for us.

The first thing in there for us is a release from our schoolmaster.

Galatians 3:25 *But after that faith is come, we are no longer under a schoolmaster.*

Remember that hard, rigid, impatient schoolmaster, the law? When we finally get to look into the will, we find something like this:

"I, God the Son, being of sound mind and crucified yet risen again body, do bestow to them who believe on me complete freedom from the bondage of the law."

Praise God, we are not under the law; we are under grace. God said it Himself! I will daily look to the law to find principles that will tell me what God does and does not like. I will absolutely commit to obeying every moral law, but I never have to scour the law or the traditions of the elders to figure out what meat I can and cannot eat, what feasts I must attend, or how to make my house ceremonially clean. God gave me liberty from that right there in His last will and testament.

The second thing in the will for us is a brand-new Father.

Galatians 3:26 *For ye are all the children of God by faith in Christ Jesus.*

This may not mean much to you, but as a kid who grew up without a father, it means a great deal to me. I just love looking into the last will and testament and reading something like this:

"I, God the Son, grant to those who believe on me my very own Father to be their Father."

We all had such an awful father before:

John 8:44 *Ye are of your father the devil, and the lusts of your father ye will do.*

95

But when I got saved, God gave the devil a TPR for me, a termination of parental rights. He then adopted me into His own family. I can crawl up into His lap and cry Abba, Father. It is right there in my inheritance papers; I have been granted the Father of Jesus to be my Father too.

The third thing in the will for us is a new identity.

Galatians 3:27 *For as many of you as have been baptized into Christ have put on Christ.*

When this speaks of being "*baptized into Christ*," it is not referring to water baptism. It is referring to dying with Him as a sinner:

Romans 6:3 *Know ye not, that so many of us as were baptized into Jesus Christ were baptized into his death?*

This is talking about getting saved, having the old man that we once were die, and being born again a new creature in Christ. When we do that, we have "*put on Christ*." In other words, when God the Father sees us, He sees His own dear Son instead of us, and He is satisfied with us. It is right there in His last will and testament for us:

"I, God the Son, do grant to those who believe in me the exact same holiness, righteousness, and goodness that I myself have. I grant them my very own identity!"

When people go into the witness protection program, they are given a new identity, a fresh start. But that does not even begin to compare to the fresh start that God gives us. Those things you did before you got saved, you did not do them. The person that did them died when you got saved, and you have been covered in Christ ever since. What a great new identity!

The fourth thing in the will for us is equal status with every believer.

Galatians 3:28 *There is neither Jew nor Greek, there is neither bond nor free, there is neither male nor female: for ye are all one in Christ Jesus.*

Is God saying here that there are literally no more Jews, literally no more Gentiles, literally no more men, women, slaves, or free people? Obviously not. What he was saying is that before Christ came, the Jews had a much higher status than the Gentiles, men had a much higher status than women, and free men had a much higher status than slaves. But once people get saved, they find themselves standing on the level ground of the cross of Calvary because those distinctions grant no preference at all when it comes to salvation or the blessings that spring from it.

It is right there in His last will and testament for us:

"I, God the Son, do bequeath to those who believe in me, equal status with every believer of every age. I grant to them the status of Paul, and Peter, and Moses, and Abraham, and David, and Elijah. I grant that they all may be one."

The fifth and final thing in the will for us is to be made an equal heir with Abraham, and thus with Christ Himself.

Galatians 3:29 *And if ye be Christ's, then are ye Abraham's seed, and heirs according to the promise.*

Another verse that describes this even more plainly is:

Romans 8:17 *And if children, then heirs; heirs of God, and joint-heirs with Christ; if so be that we suffer with him, that we may be also glorified together.*

He will always be the Son that God the Father prizes above all because of what He did on Calvary. But He so prizes His Son that, when the Son asks to have us as joint heirs, the Father willingly allows it. He will spend eternity in heaven, and so will we. He will be glorified, and so will we. He will never suffer again, and neither will we. It is right there in His last will and testament for us:

"I, God the Son, give to those who believe in me the right of being a joint heir with me. What is mine will also be theirs."

What an inheritance! We have it all, and it is all through placing our faith in the Lord Jesus Christ. The law never did anything like that for us!

In 1626, Peter Minuit, director of the Dutch Settlement, sat down with the Lenni Lenape Indians, who lived on the land that is known now as Manhattan, New York. That land today is quite literally the most valuable land on earth. In fact, in pure real estate value, that land, just the land itself, not the buildings, is worth about 1.4 trillion dollars today. But when Peter Minuit sat down with the Lenni Lenape, he had an offer for them that they just could not refuse. He was willing to buy that land from them for the enormous price of... about $24.00 worth of plastic beads and trinkets. They sold him the land! They gave up one of the most valuable inheritances ever for a handful of trinkets. (Yglesias, 2016)

As bad as that is, it is not nearly as bad as a child of God who could look at the inheritance we have because of simple faith in Christ and then trade away that inheritance for the plastic beads of the works of the law.

Chapter Eight
Who's Your Daddy?

Galatians 4:1 *Now I say, That the heir, as long as he is a child, differeth nothing from a servant, though he be lord of all;* **2** *But is under tutors and governors until the time appointed of the father.* **3** *Even so we, when we were children, were in bondage under the elements of the world:* **4** *But when the fulness of the time was come, God sent forth his Son, made of a woman, made under the law,* **5** *To redeem them that were under the law, that we might receive the adoption of sons.* **6** *And because ye are sons, God hath sent forth the Spirit of his Son into your hearts, crying, Abba, Father.* **7** *Wherefore thou art no more a servant, but a son; and if a son, then an heir of God through Christ.*

There is a phrase that has been around for a long time, a phrase normally used as a put-down. When someone beats you in arm wrestling, they will say, "Who's your daddy?" When a wide receiver catches a touchdown pass, he will often go to the cornerback that was covering him and say, "Who's your daddy?" It is a way for the antagonist to imply that they are the daddy, and you are just a snot-nosed little punk; they are in charge, and you have to do whatever they say.

That physical putdown is originally from the attitude of a spiritual entity. It is the attitude of the devil himself; when you get right down to it, he really thinks he is better than you. He thought he was better than God, so, of course, he thinks he is better than you!

It is also the attitude of the devil's religious crowd, people that believe that salvation is by works. They also believe that they are better than you and that you ought to bow down and do whatever they say. The Judaizers held that exact same attitude towards the Galatians. In effect, they were saying, "Hey, you heathen Gentile Galatians, who's your daddy?" And in Galatians chapter four, Paul told them exactly how to answer that question.

The Trials of Puberty

Have you ever heard the statement, "Too much of a good thing?" I think I can illustrate it for you. If I asked an honest older person, "Would you like to be young again?" they would say, "Sure!" But if I then said, "Okay, how about eleven years old?" They would say, "Not on your life!" They may want to be young again, but I promise you they do not want to be that young again because they remember what it was like the first time around!

That very type of thought is brought up by Paul in the very first verses of chapter four.

Galatians 4:1 *Now I say, That the heir, as long as he is a child, differeth nothing from a servant, though he be lord of all; 2 But is under tutors and governors until the time appointed of the father.*

The word child in verse one indicates the time from toddlerhood to pre-adulthood. A good portion of that time is what we would today call "puberty." And it is a hard time to deal with!

Now, you might think that being an heir to a wealthy family would make it easier. But according to Paul, that is not so. You see, a child may be the heir to the family fortune and as such the "lord of all," but as long as he is still a kid, he is really no better than the hired servants. They are not in charge; he is not in charge. They have to depend on the adults; he has to depend on the adults. Until that child finally grows up, he really does not have it nearly as good as he is one day going to have it.

But what in the world does this have to do with Judaizers, Gentile Christians, salvation by grace instead of by works, all of the things that Paul has been dealing with? Has he gone off-subject? No, he is still very much on subject. He explains his illustration in the next verse:

Galatians 4:3 *Even so we, when we were children, were in **bondage** under the elements of the world:*

Look again at the verse that gives the theme for the book of Galatians, and notice the common word that appears both there and here in Galatians 4:3.

Galatians 5:1 *Stand fast therefore in the liberty wherewith Christ hath made us free, and be not entangled again with the yoke of **bondage**.*

Paul knew that the Galatians used to be in bondage; he himself once had been as well. And he did not want them to go back. And this brings up a question that we need to deal with. If these were saved Gentiles, how is it that Paul is reminding them that they were, past tense, in bondage under the elements of the world, meaning the Jewish law? The simple answer is that they were heathens who converted to Judaism and who later got saved and became Christians. This would also explain why the Judaizers were so anxious to get them back in the fold; it looked very bad for them to lose their converts to Paul and Christ and Christianity!

Again, the elements of the world that Paul spoke of in verse three are, as Adam Clarke comments, "the rudiments or principles of the Jewish religion." (403) Paul is saying that there was a time when the Galatian believers were in bondage under these elements of the world, and he did not want them to go back to that time and place themselves under that bondage again. That time was the time before they came to know Christ when the law held sway over them. And this was the time that the Judaizers kept looking back to with such fondness! The Judaizers wanted to go back to the way it was before Calvary, and they wanted to take the Galatians with them. They wanted the Galatians to go back to spiritual puberty.

If I suddenly developed the miraculous ability to not only go back to puberty but to touch people on the head and take them back with me, every adult in the world would scream like a girl when they saw me coming their way. But the Galatians, hearing that foolish pitch from the Judaizers, were saying, "Give up the freedom of our spiritual adulthood in Christ and go back to spiritual puberty? Wow, that sounds like a great idea!"

But it is not. And anyone who wants to get you back under the law, under the customs and traditions of the elders, is trying to do the same thing to you, trying to take you back to spiritual puberty. Don't go! You must get over the idea that things were better under the law. They were not. I would not go back and live under Moses for a single second. I thank God for Calvary, and I thank God that I live after Calvary! Do not ever let anyone take you back and put you under the law. That was the time of spiritual puberty, and we are all grown up now.

The Time of Placement

Galatians 4:4 *But when the fulness of the time was come, God sent forth his Son, made of a woman, made under the law,*

But when the fulness of the time was come—what an amazing phrase. Listen to Adam Clark eloquently describe "the fulness of the time:"

> "The time which God in his infinite wisdom counted best; in which all his counsels were filled up; and the time which his Spirit, by the prophets, had specified; and the time to which he intended the Mosaic institutions should

extend, and beyond which they should be of no avail." (403)

That is very good, but let me give a much simpler description of "the fulness of the time:"

At just the right moment, when the world was starving to death for something truly satisfying, when people in spiritual bondage were begging for liberty, God sent forth His Son.

...when the fulness of the time was come, God sent forth his Son, made of a woman...

Anyone who knows anything at all about their Bible understands exactly what "made of a woman" means. Jesus Christ did not have an earthly father. He was virgin conceived, virgin born. He was the fulfillment of Genesis 3:15 and Isaiah 7:14. Joseph was not the father, a Roman soldier was not the father, God the Father was the Father of the Son that God the Holy Spirit lovingly placed into Mary's womb.

...when the fulness of the time was come, God sent forth his Son, made of a woman, made under the law...

Made under the law. What is that about? Just this: the law held all mankind in an iron grip. That hold could only be broken from the inside out. In order for the hold of the law to be broken for mankind, someone had to be under the law, fulfill all of the law perfectly, and then give that righteousness to those who had been unrighteous. In His lifetime, Jesus did what no one else ever could do. In his actions, attitudes, and intentions, He fulfilled the law perfectly. As His last act of fulfilling the law, He went and hung on the tree so He could be made a curse for us so that He could make an essential transfer. On Calvary, He transferred our sin onto Himself and His righteousness onto us. He came under the law so He could break us out from under the law. The law was killing us, and He was the only one who could save us. The very next thing that we read verifies that:

Galatians 4:5 *To redeem them that were under the law...*

103

To redeem means to "buy something back." When God made man in the garden, we belonged to Him; He was our Father. He bought us the first time by making us. When man sinned and fell, we became the children of the devil, in bondage under the law. So Jesus went to Calvary, and with His own blood, He bought us back. We were worthless, scarred, and stained, but He loved us so much that He paid the ultimate price to have us again and to have us forever.

But He did not buy us back so we could be children again. Look at the last half of this verse:

...To redeem them that were under the law, that we might receive the adoption of sons.

Do you remember that word "child" from verse one and "children" from verse three? That applied to what we were under the law before Calvary. There is a very different word used for us here. God did not come and die so that we could be children anymore; He came so that He could give us "*the adoption of sons.*" That phrase means "To be placed in the family as an adult son with all of the blessings and benefits that go with it."

So in the perfect time, God came to make us the perfect age. We are no longer little children looking back to Mount Sinai to find out what kind of fabrics we can and cannot use in our clothing, but adult sons looking back to Mount Calvary where Jesus gave us robes of purest white, made so by the blood of the Lamb!

Please do not misunderstand me or Paul. The Old Testament is still God's Word, and it is still relevant. Romans 15:4 says that it was written for our learning. Much of it was restated for us in the New Testament. Jesus restated nine of the ten commandments for us, everything except the keeping of the Sabbath day, which was specifically for the Jews (Exodus 31:16-17), even though many of the principles of the Sabbath day are properly carried over into Sunday, the Lord's day. But the ceremonial law was fulfilled in Christ and at Calvary and is no longer needed. The civil law was for Israel as an Old Testament nation and is no longer needed. If you really want to know where to look to find out how a Christian should conduct his everyday life, your *primary* search will be from Matthew to Revelation, your *secondary* search will be from Genesis to Malachi, and you will have to keep in mind the fact that the New Testament will be the rule as to which parts of the Old Testament law are still in some way binding for our behavior today!

The Truth Paternal

Can we agree that daytime television is a vast wasteland of filth? First are the soaps, which are all so dirty that they shouldn't have "soap" anywhere in the name. And then there are the talk shows. All of them have their own little thing that they do for pure titillation. There is a guy named Maury Povich, and he often does paternity tests on people to determine who the father of a child is. He is trying to arrive at a "truth paternal." But in a non-lurid way, Paul was trying to demonstrate the same thing to the Galatians:

Galatians 4:6 *And because ye are sons, God hath sent forth the Spirit of his Son into your hearts, crying, Abba, Father.*

Notice that first phrase, *"because ye are sons."* This is a settled issue. If you are saved, you are what you have never been before, a child of God. Your entire family status has changed. The devil, through the years, doubtless enjoyed yanking you around by a chain when you were lost. He loved sticking that long forked tongue in your face, with breath straight from the pits of hell, and saying, "Hey, boy, who's your daddy?" And all those years, you, in honesty, had to hang your head and say, "You are, Satan, you are."

But then one day, some of you reading this book knelt down, perhaps at an altar, wet that altar with bitter tears, begged God for forgiveness, had sweet peace flood your soul, and became that very day a child of God. And if you think back to it, you will probably realize that after that, the devil did not ask you that question anymore. He decided to "drop the subject." But why should we let him get by with dropping the subject when it finally gets fun to talk about? Now would be a good time to say, "Hey, devil! Ask me again! Ask me who my Daddy is now!"

Because ye are sons, says verse six, God hath sent forth the Spirit of His Son into your heart crying, Abba, Father.

Follow this carefully. The fact that you are sons is the reason why God does what He says He does here, sending the Spirit of His Son into your heart crying, Abba, Father. Let me tell you what this means. Jesus the Son already knows how to behave like the Son of God. He has been the Son of God for all eternity past. He knows what privileges He has as the Son of God. But the thing is, we do not! When we get saved, we are new to this thing of being a son or daughter of God. We have no real clue what our rights and privileges are. We have never had God as our Father before. Our tendency, therefore, may be to be shy, reserved, and just hang back. Our tendency may be just to be happy that we are inside the door of salvation and curl up just inside the door.

But when God the Son sees that, when He sees us curled up just inside the door, not moving further inside, He comes by, takes us by the hand, and says, "This just won't do. You do not see me acting like that, do you? Come with me."

And Jesus, the Son of God, leads us right into the heart of the spiritual mansion, enters the room where God the Father is sitting in His giant chair, crawls up in the Father's lap, and brings us with Him. Jesus is not content just to see us saved and escaping hell; He will not be satisfied until we have made ourselves just as at home with the Father as He is!

Do you want to know how intimate that becomes? Look at verse six again:

Galatians 4:6 *And because ye are sons, God hath sent forth the Spirit of his Son into your hearts, crying, Abba, Father.*

Abba is not a Hebrew word but a Syriac word, and it denotes filial affection. It is a term of tenderness and closeness. In our modern vernacular, it would be far less formal than father and more akin to "dad."

We can easily understand how Jesus could use that term with the Father, but the Father wants us to be that close to Him as well! The Son can think of Him as dad, and as amazing as it is, so can we. When the devil is giving us fits, we can legitimately say something like, "Who's my daddy? God the Father is my Daddy! Don't mess with me; you don't know my daddy!"

Notice also that it is the Spirit of Jesus in us crying Abba. When we cry "Dad!" to the Father, it is Jesus' voice He hears. No wonder we are allowed such a familiarness with Him!

Galatians 4:7 *Wherefore thou art no more a servant, but a son; and if a son, then an heir of God through Christ.*

When mankind was under the law, we were nothing more than servants, slaves, people under bondage. But when you get saved, you are no more a servant under the bondage of the law; you are a child of the King, an heir of God because of what Jesus did on Calvary. This is the status that the Galatian believers had. They were sons of God! They were no longer common slaves under the bondage of the law. They could crawl up into God's lap along with Jesus and say, "Dad! My Father!"

But then some human beings, some children of Satan, came by and, in so many words, said, "Get out of God's lap. Who do you think you are? I'll tell you who you are; you're a slave. Put this yoke of bondage back on. Get out there into the field with the rest of the bondslaves."

And they did! They went out and started getting circumcised, keeping the Sabbath, memorizing the commands of the elders, and keeping the feast days. What they should have done is said, "I don't think so! You go out into the field with the bondslaves. You wear the yoke of bondage. I have been adopted; I am free; I am a son of God. God is my Abba, Father, so do not ever, ever act like my spiritual father when it is clear that you are not even saved."

Here is how the Gaithers so poetically put this concept in musical form:

"My father is rich, in houses and lands, He holdeth the wealth of the world in His hands, of rubies and diamonds of silver and gold, His coffers are full, He has riches untold.

I'm a child of the King, a child of the King, with Jesus my Savior, I'm a child of the King."

If you are saved, you really are a child of the King. So why would you ever trade such liberty and access for the slavery you left behind?

Chapter Nine
Weak and Beggarly Elements

Galatians 4:8 *Howbeit then, when ye knew not God, ye did service unto them which by nature are no gods. 9 But now, after that ye have known God, or rather are known of God, how turn ye again to the weak and beggarly elements, whereunto ye desire again to be in bondage? 10 Ye observe days, and months, and times, and years. 11 I am afraid of you, lest I have bestowed upon you labour in vain. 12 Brethren, I beseech you, be as I am; for I am as ye are: ye have not injured me at all. 13 Ye know how through infirmity of the flesh I preached the gospel unto you at the first. 14 And my temptation which was in my flesh ye despised not, nor rejected; but received me as an angel of God, even as Christ Jesus. 15 Where is then the blessedness ye spake of? for I bear you record, that, if it had been possible, ye would have plucked out your own eyes, and have given them to me. 16 Am I therefore become your enemy, because I tell you the truth? 17 They zealously affect you, but not well; yea, they would exclude you, that ye might affect them. 18 But it is good to be zealously affected always in a good thing, and not only when I am present with you.*

Way back in the day when I ran my jewelry store, I remember a guy coming in with a huge smirk on his face like he had just discovered the world's best secret. He took a chain off of his neck, laid it down on the counter for me, and said, "What do you think of that? Your gold chains are $200-$300, and I just bought this off a guy down the street for $80.00."

I picked up the chain, looked at it, and said, "I think you spent about $79.00 too much. This isn't gold."

He said, "But it's stamped 14k!"

I went to the back and brought out my own 14k stamp. I said, "Anybody on earth can buy one of these for about $20.00 and stamp whatever they want. I could stamp my cat 14k, but it wouldn't make it so. This isn't gold; it isn't even silver covered in gold; it's just pot metal colored yellow; it has absolutely no value."

You should have seen that guy take off back down the street, trying to catch the "bargain jewelry salesman" to get his $80.00 back!

There are things in life that are so shiny and pretty and look so nice but have no value at all to them! The same truth applies in the spiritual realm. People often spend a spiritual fortune on shiny things of absolutely no value. Paul called them weak and beggarly elements.

A Great Lack

Galatians 4:8 *Howbeit then, when ye knew not God, ye did service unto them which by nature are no gods.* **9** *But now, after that ye have known God, or rather are known of God, how turn ye again to the weak and beggarly elements, whereunto ye desire again to be in bondage?*

We start this section with the word "howbeit." In this verse, it basically means, "how is it?" It points back to who our Father is in the first seven verses and all the blessings that we have as sons of God that we could never have had when we were in bondage under the law. Paul was saying, "How is it that you went from being heathens, serving false Gods, converted to Judaism and ended up under the bondage of the law, then finally got saved and experienced the truth and the freedom of Christ, yet have now decided to go back into bondage again? How is it that now that you have finally known God, or to put it more properly, how is it that after God has finally known you as dear sons, how is it that you want to give all of those blessings up?"

The words that Paul used are powerful. He said, "You want to go back to weak and beggarly elements." Weak means "having no power," and beggarly means "having no value." Works for salvation have absolutely no power and absolutely no value!

Baptism in its proper place is a good thing. But if you think baptism can save you or even help to save you, then you are trusting in something with no value and no power.

Church membership in its proper place is a good thing. But if you think that can save you or even help to save you, then you are trusting in something with no value and no power.

Tithing in its proper place is a good thing. But if you think that can save you or even help to save you, then you are trusting in something with no value and no power.

If you want to worship on Saturday, go ahead, it is not a sin. But if you think that can save you or even help to save you, then you are trusting in something with no value and no power.

Spending a lifetime on the streets of Calcutta feeding orphans is a good thing. But if you think that can save you or even help to save you, then you are trusting in something with no value and no power.

Salvation is by repenting of your sin and placing your faith in the Lord Jesus Christ.

The Galatians had some particular parts of the law they were being drawn back into. Paul spelled out some of them in the next verse:

Galatians 4:10 *Ye observe days, and months, and times, and years.*

To observe means "to keep scrupulously, to neglect nothing requisite to the religious observance of the thing or day." In other words, they had gone full-bore back into the keeping of the Old Testament Jewish feasts and ceremonies. Every special day, every sacred month, every significant year. Do you realize what that means? If you look at what the Jewish calendar had become by then, it means that pretty much all day every day was some special Jewish thing for them to do. They didn't have time to be Christians anymore; they were living like full-time Jews!

There was the Sabbath every single week. There was the feast of mixtures. There was the Passover. There was the feast of shekels. There was the Day of Atonement. There was the feast of Tabernacles. There was the feast of the Egg. There was Rosh Hashanah. There was Ta-anith, the time of fasting. There was Purim. There was the feast of irrigation. There was the feast of weeks. There was the seventh year of release, then there was the fiftieth year of Jubilee. There were high holy days. There were days of observance for great heroes and events of the past. There were special days called for mourning and the affliction of one's soul. The list went on forever.

These Galatians had gotten saved, they had been spending their days reading their Bibles and praying and soul-winning and praising God for what Jesus did on Calvary and rejoicing over their heavenly home to come, and then they gave it all up to place themselves under the bondage of the Jewish religious calendar, something that as far as salvation is concerned is of no value and no power. The real value and power of those feasts and days are that the ones that God instituted pointed to the Lord Jesus Christ. Their proper value was something for us to look at to see and understand the work and person of Christ more clearly!

A Great Labor

Galatians 4:11 *I am afraid of you, lest I have bestowed upon you labour in vain.*

Let me paraphrase this for you. Paul was saying, "You scare me because I am beginning to think that I worked so hard to see you get saved, but you might not have really gotten saved after all. Maybe you got emotional, maybe you got stirred, but I am beginning to wonder whether you really got born again."

I know how Paul felt. Every good pastor does. I know how it feels to labor and witness and pray for someone, then see that person come down to the altar and make a profession of faith, but then later see that person go right back to their old ways. I know what it is like to lay awake at night praying, "O Lord, if they didn't really get saved, please let them know! God, I do not want them going to hell while they are convinced they are going to heaven."

Galatians 4:12 *Brethren, I beseech you, be as I am; for I am as ye are: ye have not injured me at all.*

I mean no disrespect at all, but this is one of those verses that has a little bit of a Dr. Seuss ring to it. Paul is basically saying this:

"I was a Jew, but I became like you. But then you see, you became like me. Let that be through, become more like you."

In other words, Paul was reminding them that when he, a Jew, got saved, he gave up the Jewish rites and ceremonies. He ignored them just like the Gentiles had all along. But then these Gentiles that he had won to God turned around and started acting like Jews, following all the rites and customs that Paul himself had given up. You had a Jew acting like Gentiles, and Gentiles acting like Jews, and Paul was saying, "Let's get together on this thing. Come back to where I am at, come back to where you used to be, come back to just believing that what Jesus did is sufficient."

I love the way he closed that thought in verse twelve: "*Ye have not injured me at all.*" Have you ever heard the old saying, "It's no skin off my nose"? This basically means the same thing. They weren't hurting Paul by what they were doing; they were only hurting themselves.

A Great Love

Galatians 4:13 *Ye know how through infirmity of the flesh I preached the gospel unto you at the first.* **14** *And my temptation which was in my flesh ye despised not, nor rejected; but received me as an angel of God, even as Christ Jesus.*

When I was working on my undergraduate degree in Bible College, I sometimes received some very good advice, but at other times I got some very bad advice. One piece of bad advice I remember getting was this: never get close to your people. Right off the bat, I knew that just was not Biblical. Jesus got close enough to His people to have John lay his head on His chest. He got close enough to call even Judas "friend." He got close enough to take the little children up in His arms. He got close enough to send his own mother home with John as He was dying.

The only way I can see to pastor people without getting close to them is to not really pastor them. It is hard to weep over the coffin of a loved one with people and not get close to them. It is hard to spend hours in a surgical waiting room and not get close to people. It is hard to crawl under houses and fix busted water pipes and not get close to people. It is hard to go out to dinner and laugh and cut up and fellowship and not get close to people. It is hard to spend months wiring a building together and not get close to people. It is hard to help people through legal battles and not get close to them. It is hard to pray over ruined homes and wayward kids and not get close to people. It is hard to win people to the Lord, teach them and train them, and not get close to them.

I understand the risks full well. And truthfully, there have been a lot of times that I regretted getting close to people just because of the pain that eventually came from it. But Paul got close to the Galatians. He loved them, and there was a time they loved him.

If you look at verse thirteen, you will see that when Paul got to Galatia, he was not doing well physically. He had an infirmity in his flesh. If you think back to his missionary journeys, this is not hard to believe. Everywhere he went, he was getting stoned or beaten with rods or chained in a dungeon or attacked by a mob or whipped and scourged. Paul was a physical wreck. He showed up in Galatia, not in a three-piece suit with perfectly coiffed hair and freshly manicured nails and a Colgate smile; he showed up looking like he had fallen out of the top of the ugly tree and hit every single branch on the way down.

But they loved him. He told them about Jesus. He won them to God; he brought them the message that rescued them from an eternity in hell. They looked at him like he was an angel of God; they treated him with the same kindness they would have treated Jesus Himself.

Galatians 4:15 *Where is then the blessedness ye spake of? for I bear you record, that, if it had been possible, ye would have plucked out your own eyes, and have given them to me.*

This verse lets us know a little bit more about Paul and about how much the Galatians loved him. Throughout the account of Paul, we get hints of the fact that he had a serious eye problem. He was blinded on the road to Damascus, and even though God gave him back his sight, it looks as though it may have impacted him later. In chapter six of this book, Paul will basically allude to the fact that he wrote in very big letters, likely because of that horrible eyesight.

The Galatians saw his eye problem, and they literally loved this man so much that if it had been possible, they would have plucked out their own eyes and given them to him. But oh, how things changed.

Galatians 4:16 *Am I therefore become your enemy, because I tell you the truth?*

I do not think there is any hurt worse than this one. To pour your life into people, sacrifice so much for them, and then have them turn on you because you tell them the truth; that hurts deeply.

These Judaizers did not just undermine the message of Paul; in so doing, they ruined the Galatians' relationship with Paul. They made the Galatians look at the best friend they ever had like he was their enemy.

Galatians 4:17 *They zealously affect you, but not well; yea, they would exclude you, that ye might affect them.*

Once again, let me paraphrase this verse for you to give you a sense of what it means: "Those Judaizers are having a really big impact on you, but it isn't a good impact. They are getting you all stirred up, but for all the wrong reasons. They want to exclude you from the simple grace of Christ so that you can have a big impact on them. They want you as trophies to wave around for all their buddies back in Jerusalem. They are not in it for you; they are in it for themselves."

If you have ever been around a preacher who is in it for himself, you know what this is like. If you have ever been around a preacher who thought that you were there for him instead of him being there for you, you know the arrogance these Judaizers had. You know how they were using the Galatians.

That is a bitter form of bondage when you find yourself enslaved not just to traditions and customs and laws but also to a man who looks at you like a personal bondslave.

Galatians 4:18 *But it is good to be zealously affected always in a good thing, and not only when I am present with you.*

The first half of this verse is one that a great many of today's "normal church crowd," if they were honest, would have to admit that they do not like and maybe do not even believe in.

Paul said, "*it is good to be zealously affected always in a good thing*," and almost in unison, the Pharisaical wing of mainstream Christianity says, "SHHHHH! No, it isn't! Let all things be done decently and in order. Zeal is nothing more than shallow emotionalism. Stop smiling. Stop shouting. Stop crying. Stop raising your hands in worship. Stop coming to the altar before the official invitation. Have a strict schedule and keep to it. Never let anything like the moving of the Holy Spirit disrupt what you have already planned out well in advance."

I have an answer for that. "It is good to be zealously affected always in a good thing."

When Paul was there with them, they were all about the blood, all about grace, all about the liberty that was in Christ. They were on fire for God. But as soon as he left, the Pharisee Fire Department showed up and squirted three entire tanker loads of ice-cold water on that spiritual fire. They left the Galatians dripping wet, cold as ice, and taught them to like it. They stopped loving God, stopped loving Paul, and stopped loving the liberty that salvation had given them.

When people have been squirted down like that, it can take a while to get them dried off and ready to blaze again. Sometimes you have to fan it until you remember what it is you used to have, and you wonder why you ever let it go, especially for a bunch of weak and beggarly elements. So fan it! You ought to enjoy what Christ has afforded you because it is so much better than the weak and beggarly elements mere religion can offer!

Chapter Ten
The Children of Promise

Galatians 4:19 *My little children, of whom I travail in birth again until Christ be formed in you, 20 I desire to be present with you now, and to change my voice; for I stand in doubt of you. 21 Tell me, ye that desire to be under the law, do ye not hear the law? 22 For it is written, that Abraham had two sons, the one by a bondmaid, the other by a freewoman. 23 But he who was of the bondwoman was born after the flesh; but he of the freewoman was by promise. 24 Which things are an allegory: for these are the two covenants; the one from the mount Sinai, which gendereth to bondage, which is Agar. 25 For this Agar is mount Sinai in Arabia, and answereth to Jerusalem which now is, and is in bondage with her children. 26 But Jerusalem which is above is free, which is the mother of us all. 27 For it is written, Rejoice, thou barren that bearest not; break forth and cry, thou that travailest not: for the desolate hath many more children than she which hath an husband. 28 Now we, brethren, as Isaac was, are the children of promise. 29 But as then he that was born after the flesh persecuted him that was born after the Spirit, even so it is now. 30 Nevertheless what saith the scripture? Cast out the bondwoman and her son: for the son of the bondwoman shall not be heir with the son of the* *freewoman.* **31** *So then, brethren, we are not children of the bondwoman, but of the free.*

Most of the time, children are not perceptive enough to truly understand the ramifications of the things they desire. And that is why God gave them these wonderful things called parents. Parents have been around longer; they are more experienced, they know more, they are invaluable guides to any child that will truly listen. And Paul is now going to assume the parental role with the Galatians, hoping to get them to understand the trouble they are asking for.

An Unhappy Parent

Galatians 4:19 *My little children, of whom I travail in birth again until Christ be formed in you,* **20** *I desire to be present with you now, and to change my voice; for I stand in doubt of you.*

When Paul called the Galatians "my little children," he let us in on something that many people will never understand. When you win somebody to God, it is very much like having and raising a child. When someone gets saved, they are a babe in Christ. The real soul-winner is one who will win someone to God and then take responsibility for helping that babe to grow and mature.

Paul did this. If there was ever a man who took his spiritual parenting responsibilities seriously, he was it. He won these Galatians, he loved them, and he trained them.

Mothers who are reading this book, I have a question. Did you enjoy the hard labor part? If God miraculously gave you the ability to do so, would you go back to the day of your child or children's birth and do all of the hours of hard labor all over again? I am assuming that the answer to that question is a resounding "No!"

Paul had an issue with the Galatians. He went through the spiritual labor to have them born into the family of God, and what they were doing was making him have to go through it all again to see them brought back to where they should be spiritually. He said, "*I travail in birth again.*" They had gotten to a place where, as verse one further says, Christ was not "formed" in them. That word "formed" is the word we get our English word "morphed" from. In other words, Paul wanted Christ to be fully taking shape inside of them so they would be living like Him on the outside. The Galatians' new enslavement to the law was keeping them from becoming Christ-filled on the inside and Christ-like on the outside.

Paul said, "I wish I was present with you right now so I could change my voice." You parents, have you ever "changed your voice" with one of your bone-headed children?

Back in March of 2008, when we had already been working for two years on building our new church building, I was priming the doors in the ladies' restroom, and it dawned on me I was hearing "whacking" noises behind me. I turned around to see that my young son had placed a metal nut on the tile floor and was whacking it with a hammer, trying to flatten it. Believe me, I changed my voice with him!

Paul wanted to change his voice with the Galatians out of concern, out of fear, because he stood in doubt of them. That phrase means that he was unsure of their spiritual condition. Maybe they had not really been saved; maybe they were just backslidden; he just was not sure. Paul was one unhappy spiritual parent!

An Unwise Choice

Galatians 4:21 *Tell me, ye that desire to be under the law, do ye not hear the law?* **22** *For it is written, that Abraham had two sons, the one by a bondmaid, the other by a freewoman.* **23** *But he who was of the bondwoman was born after the flesh; but he of the freewoman was by promise.*

121

What Abraham did in his sin with Hagar was awful, and it has led to three thousand years' worth of fighting between the Jews and the Arabs. But there is at least one good thing that came from it. A thousand or so years later, Paul was able to use what happened as a spiritual lesson for the Galatians. Paul basically said, "Do you really want to be under the law? Do you think that it is a good idea to follow these Judaizers? Maybe you ought to go back and re-read the law, the law all the way back to Abraham's time because there was a law even then. Not the law of Moses, but definitely a law, and definitely recorded in the books of the law by Moses who wrote the books of the law."

Abraham had two sons. One was by Sarah, the freewoman. The other was by Hagar, the bondslave. Ishmael, son of Hagar, was born after the flesh. It was not God's idea for Abraham to sleep with Hagar; it was Sarah's idea for this to happen. In other words, Ishmael was the result of the best works and ideas of the flesh.

But Isaac, son of Sarah, was a miracle of grace. His birth defied human logic and comprehension and brought all the glory to God. That is why the promise came through Isaac, not Ishmael. In desiring to go back under the law, the Galatians were placing themselves under the likeness of Ishmael, not Isaac.

Understand this: as a bondslave, Hagar could never produce a free-born child. The best she could ever hope for was to produce a child that was just as much in bondage as she was. And this reminds us that the law can never produce freedom. All it can produce is spiritual bondage and people who are under spiritual bondage.

Galatians 4:24 *Which things are an allegory: for these are the two covenants; the one from the mount Sinai, which gendereth to bondage, which is Agar.* **25** *For this Agar is mount Sinai in Arabia, and answereth to Jerusalem which now is, and is in bondage with her children.* **26** *But Jerusalem which is above is free, which is the mother of us all.*

The first thing we need to look at is that phrase *"which things are an allegory."* Do not ever make the mistake of thinking that this means that it did not literally happen. Please remember that an allegory can be either fictional or historical and literal. An allegory is simply something that represents something else. Abraham, Sarah, Hagar, Ishmael, Isaac, and the entire historical account were very real. But that entire episode also represented a spiritual truth.

So now let us look at the allegory itself, as stated by Paul.

There are two covenants referred to: the covenant of the law that the Judaizers were promoting and the covenant of grace that Paul was promoting. The covenant of the law is represented in the allegory by Hagar and by Mount Sinai, where the law was given by Moses. Another level of this allegory is that Jerusalem, also on a mountain, was the same as Hagar and the same as Mount Sinai. Hagar was under the bondage of the law, and it could never make her free. The Jews were under the bondage of the Mosaic law, and it could never make them free.

The covenant of grace was represented by Sarah and her son Isaac. Abraham and Sarah were free, and their son was thus born free. Another level of this part of the allegory is that it is also represented by the New Jerusalem. The New Jerusalem is from above; it is not bound by the law, it is free, and it is "the mother" of the saved in that allegory.

So far, the choice seems obvious! Would you rather be from Hagar or Sarah, freeborn or born into slavery, from Mount Sinai/earthly Jerusalem or from the New Jerusalem?

Galatians 4:27 *For it is written, Rejoice, thou barren that bearest not; break forth and cry, thou that travailest not: for the desolate hath many more children than she which hath an husband.*

This verse is a quote from Isaiah 54:1.

Isaiah 54:1 *Sing, O barren, thou that didst not bear; break forth into singing, and cry aloud, thou that didst not* *travail with child: for more are the children of the desolate than the children of the married wife, saith the LORD.*

These passages deal with the fact that far more Gentiles than Jews have gotten saved and become heirs of the promise. The Gentiles were barren and alienated from God. The Jews were "married to the Lord," yet the Gentiles received the grace of God and became fruitful for God, while the Jews fell in love with the law and lost sight of God. Now, all these years later, these Jews, the Judaizers, the ones who had rejected the promise, were trying to convince the Gentile Galatians to reject grace along with them.

Galatians 4:28 *Now we, brethren, as Isaac was, are the children of promise.* **29** *But as then he that was born after the flesh persecuted him that was born after the Spirit, even so it is now.*

This passage takes us back to an episode in the life and battle between Isaac and Ishmael:

Genesis 21:8 *And the child grew, and was weaned: and Abraham made a great feast the same day that Isaac was weaned.* **9** *And Sarah saw the son of Hagar the Egyptian, which she had born unto Abraham, mocking.*

These two were young, Isaac and Ishmael. From the time they were young, there was just no getting along; they were too different. And thus we find Ishmael mocking Isaac, and that episode and all of his other dealings with Isaac were serious enough that Galatians 4:29 says that he "persecuted him." These boys were never, ever going to get along.

And Paul's point was that there is also no getting along between what they represent, grace and the law. Specifically, those that hold to the law will always mock and persecute those holding to grace! They will believe they are better than you; they will point to all their good deeds, all their form and fashion, all of their religious rituals, and then say, "What do you have?" And when you tell them you have grace, just see how well that goes over!

Grace? Not good enough. You have to be "filledwiththeHolyGhostSpeakintounges." Grace? You better get baptized before you die and go to hell. Grace? What about circumcision, you unclean Gentile? Grace? I bet you are not keeping the Saturday sabbath, are you?

People that are trusting in the works of the law will never think very much of us who have just humbly trusted in the precious grace of God. They will be just like Ishmael mocking little Isaac. But we are the children of promise, not them.

Galatians 4:30 *Nevertheless what saith the scripture? Cast out the bondwoman and her son: for the son of the bondwoman shall not be heir with the son of the freewoman.* **31** *So then, brethren, we are not children of the bondwoman, but of the free.*

That takes us back again to Genesis 21:

Genesis 21:9 *And Sarah saw the son of Hagar the Egyptian, which she had born unto Abraham, mocking.* **10** *Wherefore she said unto Abraham, Cast out this bondwoman and her son: for the son of this bondwoman shall not be heir with my son, even with Isaac.* **11** *And the thing was very grievous in Abraham's sight because of his son.* **12** *And God said unto Abraham, Let it not be grievous in thy sight because of the lad, and because of thy bondwoman; in all that Sarah hath said unto thee, hearken unto her voice; for in Isaac shall thy seed be called.*

Does that sound harsh? Sarah said, "Cast them out!" and God said, "I agree!"

Now please understand, on a personal human level, this is heart-wrenching. And it was absolutely caused by Sarah's terrible suggestion and by Abraham going along with it. But the point that Paul is accurately making is that grace and law can never co-exist when it comes to salvation. You can only have

125

one, and since only grace works, cast out the law! Cast out the bondwoman and her son. Cast out the Judaizers was Paul's point. Cast out any notion that you can be saved by keeping the ten commandments or being circumcised or keeping the Sabbath or being confirmed or praying the rosary or receiving the sacraments. Cast that out! It is grace, all grace, and only grace! We are not the children of the bondwoman; we are the children of promise.

Here is a poem I wrote back in 2008 to put this contrast between grace and law in picturesque form:

Grace and Law were together again at the family reunion last year. Law saw Grace with a smile on his face and couldn't resist a sneer.

"Well, well, well, if it isn't Grace, my happy little brother, what gives you the right to be in this place? To which Grace answered, "My Mother!"

Law said, "Well, my mom's better than yours." "Is not!" "Is too!" "Is not!" "Well, let's have a contest," said Grace to Law. "We'll settle this here on the spot."

So Mama Law and Mama Grace were called to the fore that day, the rules were explained the contest began, and everything went this way:

Bad Mama Law and Good Mama Grace were to do their motherly best, to tend to the children that they had been given was the simple yet ultimate test.

Good Mama Grace started in right away, hugging and kissing her boy, she held him and loved him and gazed in his face, for he was her great daily joy.

She looked past his faults, saw only the good, she treated him like any good mama would, but over the way, what a far different sight, for who could forget Mama Law on that night?

The first thing she did was to smack her own son, then she shouted, "I know you, I know what you've done! You call yourself pure, I know better than that, you're a liar, a cheat, and a miserable rat.

"You deserve all the worst, a slow horrible death, you really should suffer, with each daily breath. You'll never be good enough, no, not for me, you're a shriveled-up branch on my great family tree."

But what happened next was all quite unexpected, for Law said, "You see? It's just as I suspected. It's clear that I have it much better than you, for my mom will do things that yours just won't do.

She's hard and precise with no mercy at all, she'll reach out to trip you then laugh when you fall! She cuts like a knife, all the way to the core, she'll rate you a failure then hurt you some more."

And Grace had to shake his head sadly and say, "If that's what you want, then just have it your way. I'll see you again at the reunion next year, I'll bring back my smile, and you bring back your sneer.

But I can't help but say to you now my sad brother, I'm glad I have mine, instead of your mother..."

Are you a child of law, or a child of promise?

Chapter Eleven
Entangled Again

Galatians 5:1 *Stand fast therefore in the liberty wherewith Christ hath made us free, and be not entangled again with the yoke of bondage.* **2** *Behold, I Paul say unto you, that if ye be circumcised, Christ shall profit you nothing.* **3** *For I testify again to every man that is circumcised, that he is a debtor to do the whole law.* **4** *Christ is become of no effect unto you, whosoever of you are justified by the law; ye are fallen from grace.* **5** *For we through the Spirit wait for the hope of righteousness by faith.* **6** *For in Jesus Christ neither circumcision availeth any thing, nor uncircumcision; but faith which worketh by love.* **7** *Ye did run well; who did hinder you that ye should not obey the truth?* **8** *This persuasion cometh not of him that calleth you.* **9** *A little leaven leaveneth the whole lump.* **10** *I have confidence in you through the Lord, that ye will be none otherwise minded: but he that troubleth you shall bear his judgment, whosoever he be.* **11** *And I, brethren, if I yet preach circumcision, why do I yet suffer persecution? then is the offence of the cross ceased.* **12** *I would they were even cut off which trouble you.* **13** *For, brethren, ye have been called unto liberty; only use not liberty for an occasion to the flesh, but by love serve one another.* **14** *For all the law is fulfilled in one word, even in this; Thou shalt love thy neighbour as thyself.* **15**

But if ye bite and devour one another, take heed that ye be not consumed one of another. **16** *This I say then, Walk in the Spirit, and ye shall not fulfil the lust of the flesh.* **17** *For the flesh lusteth against the Spirit, and the Spirit against the flesh: and these are contrary the one to the other: so that ye cannot do the things that ye would.* **18** *But if ye be led of the Spirit, ye are not under the law.*

Our first big sloppy Boxer dog was a lovable mutt named Amber. Somebody dropped her off way out in the country where we lived, and she adopted us. That dog was many things, but "bright" was not one of them. She continually made her way over to our elderly neighbors' house and frightened those frail folks to death with her bounding all around and onto them.

So we installed an invisible fence. Then I put the shock collar on her, did the training with her, and waited to see how things would go. And the answer was "not well..."

That tank of a dog would get up a full head of steam and charge the barrier. Then when it lit her up, she would lay on the ground and writhe and yowl until I went out and dragged her back inside the boundary. She did this time and again. We knew, then, that we would have to build a fence for her. But since that would take a good bit of time, in the meantime, we tied her up. We had a huge old apple tree in our yard. So I got a very long rope and tied her to it; she had tons of space to roam, even on her tether.

But when Dana and I came home that night, we found that the dog had gone clockwise around the tree about one hundred times. Her face was pressed up against the tree, she could not move so much as an inch, and she was whining for a rescue all the while still digging to go forward, thus pressing her face farther into the bark of the tree. All she would have had to do, at some point, would have been to go counterclockwise. But no, that would have been too simple. I had to grab that dog by the collar and make about one hundred laps around the tree with her going counterclockwise.

Oh, how grateful that dog was to be free! But the very next night, it was the exact same thing. That stupid dog got entangled again after I took the time to free her. And she kept on doing it, day after day after day...

I suppose when it comes right down to it, you can't fault a dumb dog for being a dumb dog and getting all tangled up after you get her loose. But if you came home and found a person in that condition, all tangled up around a tree, face pressed up against the bark, wouldn't you have a problem with that? And if you got him loose, and the very next night there he was again, face all pressed up against the tree, whining for help, wouldn't you maybe be inclined just to leave him there? Anybody that gets all tangled up after you get them loose, maybe they deserve the predicament they find themselves in!

Paul was dealing with that with the Galatians. He brought them the gospel, won them to God, got them loose from the entanglements of the law that never had helped them, and faced the consternation of later finding them all tangled up in it again!

A Standing

Galatians 5:1 *Stand fast therefore in the liberty wherewith Christ hath made us free, and be not entangled again with the yoke of bondage.*

Whenever you see the word "therefore" in the Bible, you need to find out what it is there for. This goes back to the main thought of the last chapter, that we are not the children of the bondwoman but of the free. We are not the children of law; we are the children of promise.

Because of this, Paul says, "*Stand fast*" in the liberty wherewith Christ has made us free. The way he says this is not a suggestion. He is not saying, "Now folks, just consider this. It might be a good idea for you to stand fast in the freedom Christ has given you. If you do not want to do that, it is fine, but at least consider it."

No, the word he uses here is an imperative command. He is ordering us to stay free! This matter of our liberty in Christ is not optional. We are not to allow ourselves to be entangled again.

My uncle used to be a Catholic. But not just any Catholic; he was actually an altar boy. With a little effort, he may have ended up as the Pope! He did it all. He went to confession, he prayed the Rosary, he took the sacraments. But my uncle got saved many years ago. He came out of that bondage. He does not answer to the Pope or a priest anymore; he goes directly to God to confess any sins. And when he prays, he actually talks to God instead of just repeating what someone has told him to say.

How foolish would it be for him to give away all that freedom, rejoin the Catholic Church, and kiss the Pope's ring? It would be insane! And it would also be against Paul's direct command. Whatever "religious bondage" you came out of when you got saved, whatever form of "works salvation" you abandoned, you are never ever to go back to it. You stand free in Christ; keep standing in that freedom.

A Servitude

Galatians 5:2 *Behold, I Paul say unto you, that if ye be circumcised, Christ shall profit you nothing. 3 For I testify again to every man that is circumcised, that he is a debtor to do the whole law.*

Let us take a moment to clarify this issue of circumcision. First of all, Paul is not saying that if you are circumcised, you cannot go to heaven. Paul himself, as a Jew by birth, was circumcised! Nor was Paul saying that there is no *physical* benefit to circumcision. God gave circumcision to mankind in part because of the health benefits of it. Men who are circumcised have far lower rates of certain types of cancer. Paul is dealing in this passage with full-grown Gentile men who had never been circumcised, who were being told by the Judaizers that they had to get circumcised in order to really be saved. Remember that the Galatian church was made up of people who had once been heathens, became proselytes to Judaism, and ended up getting saved when they finally heard the gospel. But since Paul taught and practiced the Great Commission, this church had gone on to win others to the Lord, other Gentiles who had never been proselytes to Judaism and thus were not circumcised. And these especially were being targeted by the Judaizers and even by the Galatian believers who had been entangled again in their bondage.

These people were already saved! They had repented of their sins, trusted Christ as their Savior, and their names were forever in the Lamb's Book of Life. Circumcision was not going to be one ounce of a spiritual profit to them.

What these Galatians did not realize was that whoever submits to circumcision hoping to be saved is not reading the fine print. As Paul reminded them in verse three, whoever does this becomes a debtor to do the whole law! The Judaizers were not telling them this. They were saying, "Look, all you have to do is be circumcised. It is that simple." But if they were going to get saved by any part of the law, they were going to have to keep the entire law!

Whenever you meet people like the Seventh Day Adventists, you are meeting people just like the Judaizers who are not telling you about the fine print. Do you want to get saved by keeping the Sabbath? One part of the law is not enough. You are also going to have to keep all of the major and minor feasts, which is going to keep you out of work for more than thirty days every year. You are also going to have to sacrifice a whole bunch of animals every month, which will probably get you into legal trouble for animal cruelty. You are also going to have to change your diet completely. Most of what we eat is against the Jewish dietary laws. Bacon and sausage and liver mush and shrimp are all out of the question. In fact, there are more than six hundred specific laws that you are going to have to live by. The Seventh Day Adventists want to cherry-pick the one law they like, but if you are going to try and get saved by law, it will have to be the law, not a law. And since no one but Christ has ever kept the entire law, you are in trouble if this is your choice!

Galatians 5:4 *Christ is become of no effect unto you, whosoever of you are justified by the law; ye are fallen from grace.*

You may be surprised to know that this is the only place in the entire Bible where the phrase "*fallen from grace*" is found. And as such, this is where you have to look to find out what it actually means.

Notice the fact that Paul has not one time warned these Galatians that they are on the verge of losing their salvation. But what he has warned them about over and over again is that they are giving up their freedom. He says here, "*Christ is become of no effect*" to them. In other words, they are saved, but it is having no practical effect on their day-to-day lives anymore because they are not living in the freedom that Christ has given them. I have been saved for forty-three years now as I sit at my desk writing this book, and I live like it. I live in the freedom that Christ has given me. But if I resign my church tomorrow, go down to the local ultra-orthodox synagogue, put on the black robe and yarmulke, and start memorizing the Torah, if I am attending their daily prayer rituals while others are smiling and laughing and rejoicing in the Lord, Christ is no longer having any practical effect in my life! I am saved, but I have fallen from grace back into the clutches of the law, and even though I am not lost, I am miserable!

Galatians 5:5 *For we through the Spirit wait for the hope of righteousness by faith.*

The third member of the Trinity, the Holy Spirit, is brought to mind in this verse. What we believe, we believe because of Him. He is the one who has taught us to wait for the hope of righteousness, meaning salvation, heaven, the entire package, exclusively through faith. There are people who believe in trying to get righteousness by works, and none of them are being taught that heresy by the Holy Spirit! The Holy Spirit always and only teaches salvation by grace through faith apart from works.

Galatians 5:6 *For in Jesus Christ neither circumcision availeth any thing, nor uncircumcision; but faith which worketh by love.*

Now Paul comes back to the issue of circumcision again. In this verse, he points out that neither being circumcised nor not being circumcised will help you with salvation. That is not the part of you God is looking at. He is looking about two feet further north to your heart to see if you have believed Him by the faith which works because He loved you and died for you.

You can either be a Christian who is free in Christ or one who is enslaved again in bondage. And the part that makes that enslavement so foolish is that Christ has already snapped all the chains! If you go back and place yourself under the law again, you are wearing broken chains; you are a slave who could be free!

A Stoppage

Galatians 5:7 *Ye did run well; who did hinder you that ye should not obey the truth?*

This is not the only time that the Bible compares the Christian life to running a race:

Hebrews 12:1 *Wherefore seeing we also are compassed about with so great a cloud of witnesses, let us lay aside every* *weight, and the sin which doth so easily beset us, and let us run with patience the race that is set before us,*

The Christian life is like a race, a marathon. It definitely is not a sprint. It is a long-term, never give up kind of thing. Paul told the Galatians, "You were running really well!" But that could be said of a great many people. Lots of people start off well and then drop out of the race or take some detour. In this case, though, the problem was that someone "hindered the runners" so that they would stop obeying the truth. That word hinder means to drive someone back.

Several years ago, two big-name college football stars went pro, Bo Jackson, a running back, and Brian Bosworth, a linebacker. Bosworth called himself "The Boz," and he carried himself with an arrogant swagger. For his part, Bo Jackson was quite simply a freak of nature. He was six foot three inches, two hundred forty pounds, and ran a 4.2-forty. That is like a truck with the speed of a Corvette.

There came a game when their two teams played each other. And there was one play in that game where Jackson's team was about ten yards from a touchdown, and Bosworth's team was trying to stop them. The play was a handoff to Jackson. He barreled straight ahead, and barreling straight his way was middle linebacker Brian Bosworth. They were both running at each other as hard as they could go. When the collision occurred, Bo Jackson basically smashed Bosworth backward and ran over his face right into the end zone. At the beginning of the play, Bosworth was running well. But Jackson "hindered him." He drove him back.

That is the spiritual picture that Paul is using here. He is saying, "Somebody came by and ran over your spiritual face and plowed you into the ground!"

Galatians 5:8 *This persuasion cometh not of him that calleth you.*

This is very simple and straightforward truth. This new doctrinal persuasion did not come from the Christ who called them. Jesus Christ never calls people into a life of bondage to the law!

Galatians 5:9 *A little leaven leaveneth the whole lump.*

This verse teaches a really big truth through a tiny illustration. Paul said, "A little leaven, a little yeast, works its way through the whole lump and makes it all rise. Just a tiny bit of yeast makes for a big fluffy roll." That is great with rolls but bad in the spiritual realm.

What he is pointing out is that by submitting to the "little thing" of circumcision, they were going to be affected in a huge way. You can never ever give a true legalist (meaning a person who says that certain works are necessary for salvation) an inch, or he will take the entire property!

Galatians 5:10 *I have confidence in you through the Lord, that ye will be none otherwise minded: but he that troubleth you shall bear his judgment, whosoever he be.*

I love the fact that Paul knew how these folks would respond to what he was writing. He said, "I have confidence in you that you will not think any other way once you read what I have written."

As a pastor, it is nice to pretty much know how people are going to respond to what you preach and teach. This is one of the benefits of staying in one place instead of changing churches every few years!

But Paul also had a word in this verse for the Judaizers. He said, *"he that troubleth you shall bear his judgment, whosoever he be."* Paul knew of the group, the Judaizers causing the problem, but he also knew that there was a "whosoever" in charge of it. He did not seem to know who, but he knew there was a who. And whoever it was, he knew they would pay the price for it. God will judge any low-life vulture that robs the

137

freedom out of Christianity by convincing people that they are still under the law!

A Scalding

This last section is going to have a few harsh but necessary scalding remarks. If you want to know why Paul was so hot at this point, the next verse will let you know.

Galatians 5:11 *And I, brethren, if I yet preach circumcision, why do I yet suffer persecution? then is the offence of the cross ceased.*

Paul had given his life to preach the gospel, and these Judaizers were running around saying, "You may not know this, but Paul has changed his mind. He is preaching circumcision now, just like us!" They were lying about him to try and suck the Galatians into their heresy because they knew the Galatians had a lot of respect for Paul. That would be about the same as someone telling all of you, "Preacher Wagner does not believe in salvation by grace anymore. He is now preaching that we all have to become Muslims, keep the five pillars, do Jihad, and make the pilgrimage to Mecca."

It would make me furious, and it made Paul furious. He said, "If I am really preaching what they say I am preaching, why do the Jews keep stoning and beating and imprisoning me wherever I go? If I was preaching what they say I am preaching, the offence of the cross would have ceased; they would like me because I am not preaching about Calvary anymore."

Do you want to know how angry Paul was? Look at the next verse:

Galatians 5:12 *I would they were even cut off which trouble you.*

Do you realize what Paul is saying here, in context? What particular part of the law has he been talking about?

Circumcision! Paul has been talking about circumcision. And it is no accident that one verse later, he says, "I wish they were cut off." That foreskin, at circumcision, is cut off and cast away as utterly useless. Paul is saying, "That's what I think of them. They need to be just like that, cut off and cast away as useless, while the body goes on without them."

That is harsh! But it was absolutely necessary; souls and liberty were at stake.

Galatians 5:13 *For, brethren, ye have been called unto liberty; only use not liberty for an occasion to the flesh, but by love serve one another.* **14** *For all the law is fulfilled in one word, even in this; Thou shalt love thy neighbour as thyself.*

Any time a preacher preaches the kind of liberty and freedom that Paul was preaching, there is always the risk of the pendulum swinging way over to one side. People could very well say, "Well, if I'm free in Christ, no one can tell me anything. No preacher has a right to tell me how to live; no verse has the right to keep me from sleeping around; no parent can tell me when to come home; I'm free!"

Paul answers that by saying, "*Use not liberty for an occasion to the flesh.*" In other words, the liberty that Christ gives is not a license to sin, as Paul made very clear in Romans 6:1. If you treat it like it is, you are just as bad as the Judaizers, only on the other end of the spectrum. Do you know what the liberty we have in Christ is to be used for? Paul said here, "*But by love, serve one another.*" The freedom that Christ gives is supposed to make us live right, do right, treat people right, think right, be kind, be sweet, have a good attitude. And if you live like that, you are actually keeping the law! Verse fourteen says:

For all the law is fulfilled in one word, even in this; Thou shalt love thy neighbour as thyself.

You literally can summarize and fulfill the entire law just in this one phrase. Think about it: if you love your neighbor as yourself, you will not kill. If you love your neighbor as yourself, you will not commit adultery with anyone or even covet to do so. If you love your neighbor as yourself, you will not bear false witness against them. If you love your neighbor as yourself, you will not worship any false god because that may help them go to hell by following you! No matter what the law, if you truly love your neighbor as yourself, you will get it right!

Galatians 5:15 *But if ye bite and devour one another, take heed that ye be not consumed one of another.*

Oftentimes, wild animals will fight until they both end up dead. There is no winner in a contest like that. In the spiritual realm, the same thing often happens. When people get out of the right fellowship with God, they will also get out of the right fellowship with each other. What this warning tells us is that what the Judaizers had done to the Galatians had resulted in the Galatians being at each other's throats. They were fighting like wild animals where they had previously been at peace with each other because they had all been on the same page doctrinally.

Do you know what is always true about Christians who are biting and devouring one another? They are not right with God, and someone is not on the right doctrinal page.

Galatians 5:16 *This I say then, Walk in the Spirit, and ye shall not fulfil the lust of the flesh.*

We often try to do the right things, but we try to do them the hard way:

A lady in my family once walked into the living room where her husband was sitting, and posed a philosophical question to him: "Do you think it's easier to push or to pull?"

He thought and thought and thought and finally said, "To push."

She took him by the hand, led him into the kitchen where he had left a drawer open, and said, "Push."

Now he could have, theoretically, crawled under the cabinet, reached up from underneath, grabbed the back of the drawer, and pulled it in. But it was so much easier just to push.

We are often guilty of trying to do the right thing but trying to do it the hard way.

We tell people, "Stay away from the lust of the flesh!" That is Biblical, and we should both practice and preach it. But just trying to stay away from the lust of the flesh, though it is right, is not the easiest way to accomplish the task. The easy way, according to this verse, is to *"Walk in the Spirit, and ye shall not fulfill the lust of the flesh."*

Do you realize, practically, what it means? It means that if we spent more time reading our Bibles, we would not have to struggle as hard against lying. If we spent more time praying, we would not have to struggle so much not to lust. If we spent more time singing and listening to the songs of Zion, we would not have to keep reminding ourselves not to be smart mouths. If we would just spend a lot of time moving towards Christ, we would automatically be moving away from wickedness! The next verse describes it another way:

Galatians 5:17 *For the flesh lusteth against the Spirit, and the Spirit against the flesh: and these are contrary the one to the other: so that ye cannot do the things that ye would.*

What he is saying makes so much sense: if you are walking in the Spirit, you will not even be able to walk in a fleshly manner. But if you are walking in the flesh, you will not be able to walk in a spiritual manner. The two are contrary to each other; you cannot do one while doing the other. He goes so far as to use the term "lust" to show how contrary these things are. It is from the word *epithumia*, and it means "the strongest of desires." The flesh strongly desires the opposite things of the Holy Spirit, and the Holy Spirit strongly desires the opposite things of the flesh. So if you walk in the Spirit, it will be impossible to walk in the flesh at the exact same time.

Galatians 5:18 *But if ye be led of the Spirit, ye are not under the law.*

An additional benefit to what Paul just said is that if you are led of the Spirit, not only will you not be able to do the works of the flesh, you will also not be able to go back under the bondage of the law. No one who is reading and praying and letting God have control in their life will ever, ever end up going back to a religious system that puts them back under the law. The fellowship with God will be too sweet; the fellowship with the people of God will be too dear. You will not be able to go back.

That big sloppy boxer dog named Amber, we eventually had to give her away. She kept getting tangled up, she could not be kept in any fence, and whenever we let her loose, she ran over to the neighbor's house and scared them with all of her jumping around.

But about a year later, I was down at the mailbox when another big sloppy boxer dog came by. I remembered hearing a car door slamming up the road a way and tires peeling out. Someone had shoved her out and driven off. She came running by, scared to death, looking for her family, and my heart broke because she reminded me so much of Amber. I called to her, and she ran like a scared rabbit. But about twenty feet past me, she stopped. She looked back at me, looked down the road in the direction the car had gone, realized she could not catch it, and then she put her belly on the ground and crawled up to me. I patted her on the head, spoke softly to her, led her up to the house, and gave her some food and water. All of our kids realized what was going on, and they piled out of the house and started loving on her.

That dog never one time had to be on a chain or in a fence. She was waiting for us by the front door every morning; she was there to greet us every night, she had two- and one-half acres to roam at will, she was as free as a bird.

If you really understand what you have in Christ, you will never want to go back to the religious bondage that kept you from Him.

Chapter Twelve
Examine Your Orchard

Galatians 5:19 *Now the works of the flesh are manifest, which are these; Adultery, fornication, uncleanness, lasciviousness,* **20** *Idolatry, witchcraft, hatred, variance, emulations, wrath, strife, seditions, heresies,* **21** *Envyings, murders, drunkenness, revellings, and such like: of the which I tell you before, as I have also told you in time past, that they which do such things shall not inherit the kingdom of God.* **22** *But the fruit of the Spirit is love, joy, peace, longsuffering, gentleness, goodness, faith,* **23** *Meekness, temperance: against such there is no law.* **24** *And they that are Christ's have crucified the flesh with the affections and lusts.* **25** *If we live in the Spirit, let us also walk in the Spirit.* **26** *Let us not be desirous of vain glory, provoking one another, envying one another.*

One thing that always disappoints me is how little emphasis people place on how they are actually living. People tend to place all their emphasis on the fact that "when I was little, I prayed and asked God to save me." But the truth is, anyone who has truly been born again will have evidence of that salvation in their life. Salvation is a drastic, dramatic, life-altering thing. There are things that it will produce in your life. This is a very good thing because it can help you to know if you have truly been born again.

The works of the flesh

Galatians 5:19 *Now the works of the flesh are manifest, which are these; Adultery, fornication, uncleanness, lasciviousness,* **20** *Idolatry, witchcraft, hatred, variance, emulations, wrath, strife, seditions, heresies,* **21** *Envyings, murders, drunkenness, revellings, and such like: of the which I tell you before, as I have also told you in time past, that they which do such things shall not inherit the kingdom of God.*

When verse nineteen says that the works of the flesh are "manifest," that word manifest means "apparent, plainly manifest and known." In other words, there just is not any doubt that these things are wrong and are produced by the flesh. If this is what you see when you look at your life, you are not saved. Verse twenty-one says that they which do such things shall not inherit the kingdom of God. That word "do" is from the word *prasso*, and it means to practice, to do, to be busy with. It is more than just stumbling into a singular act; it is a consistent behavior. A person may be able to backslide briefly into something on this list, but they will not be able to live a lifestyle of anything on this list. Only a lost person can do that. So let's look at the list that can tell a person that they are lost. And as we do, note that the word "works" in verse nineteen is plural. In other words, these are seventeen individual things, not a package deal. This will become important for us to remember when we get to the fruit of the Spirit starting in verse twenty-two.

The first item on the list is **adultery**. It is from the word *moikea*. Adultery is sex that breaks a marriage vow. If you are a single person who has sex with a married person, you have both committed adultery. If you are a married person who has sex with some other married person other than your spouse, you have both committed adultery.

Any time one married person has sex with anyone other than the person to whom they are married, two people have committed adultery. And while the world now at best simply shrugs it off and, at worst, actually celebrates it, adultery has never ceased to be a heinous evil in God's sight.

Some form of the word adultery is found nearly seventy times in Scripture. In the Old Testament, there was not even a sacrifice available for this sin; it simply brought the death penalty. Since marriage is the picture of Christ's love for the church, adultery will always be an abominable sin.

The second item on the list is **fornication**. It is from the word *porneia*, and not surprisingly, we get our word pornography from it. Fornication is an umbrella term that encompasses all forms of sexual impurities. Adultery and pre-marital sex and sodomy and bestiality and lesbianism and pornography all fall under the heading of fornication. Simply put, any sexual gratification outside of the bonds of marriage between a man and his wife is fornication.

The third item on the list is **uncleanness**. It comes from the word *akatharsia*. You may recognize our English word catharsis in that word. Catharsis is a purging or cleansing. When you put the a, the alpha privative in Greek, ahead of it, you get the opposite.

So we find here that uncleanness is one of the works of the flesh. And it is a very general term; it simply means living a dirty life in a moral sense. And the reason God puts a general term in here like that is just in case our particular dirty sin is not on this list. There are far more than just seventeen things that God views as heinous wrongs, and our society comes up with more of them by the day.

The fourth item on the list is **lasciviousness**. It is from the word *aselgia*, and it means unbridled lust, shamelessness, outrageous behavior. And that word perfectly describes our modern day. The perverted men dressing as trashy, whorish women and parading themselves in front of children in filthy drag queen story hour shows are being lascivious. The woman

145

on Twitter recently smiling and wearing a T-shirt that said, "I've had 21 abortions" is being lascivious. Teachers who discuss their sexuality with their students are being lascivious.

The fifth item on the list is **idolatry**. It comes from the word *eidolatria*, and it means worshipping something instead of God. All through the Old Testament times, Israel did this, worshipping Baal and Moloch and Ashtoreth and others.

For a while, modern man mostly laid actual statue idols aside and worshipped things like money as idols. But now, actual idol worship is making quite the comeback in our land. New York City recently put an eight-foot bronze idol on top of the new courthouse, a golden-looking woman with goat-like horns dedicated to promoting abortion. It is idolatry, plain and simple, and there are many more examples of idols being erected in our land recently.

The sixth item on the list is **witchcraft**. It is from the word *pharmakeia* from which we get our word pharmaceuticals. This is very fitting; witchcraft and drug use have always gone hand in hand. And any form of witchcraft or illicit drug use is absolutely a work of the flesh. As with adultery, witchcraft actually brought the death penalty in the Old Testament; that should tell you how serious God is about it, even though kids are being raised now to believe that it is "cool."

The seventh item on the list is **hatred**. It is from the word *echthra*, and it is very much self-defined. It is also absolutely rampant in our world. People are being actively taught to hate people based on the color of their skin. I watched a video online recently of a woman saying, "We do not intend to deconstruct the white race; we intend to completely destroy the white race. We intend to eliminate it."

It is hatred. It is one of the works of the flesh.

People are being actively taught to hate straight men. People are being actively taught to hate the Jews. People are being actively taught to hate conservatives. And such hatred is a work of the flesh.

The eighth item on the list is **variance**. It is from the word *eris*, and it means contention. It is open acts of disputing, a lifestyle of constant, intentional troublemaking. It is things like Antifa burning down cities and shooting at the police and beating innocent bystanders. It is things like the Church of Christ pastor in Virginia who takes his video camera into Baptist churches and starts arguments, and then takes the video back to his studio and edits and splices it to look horrible and puts it on television.

And it is a work of the flesh.

The ninth item on the list is **emulation**. It is from the word *dzaylos*, and in this case, it means fierce jealousy. And it can be seen everywhere in our day. If you start a business and work hard and invest and save and manage to make it big, you are going be the target of emulation, fierce jealousy. People will be demanding that the government take what you have and give it to them.

If you have a beautiful spouse and a wonderful relationship, you are going to be the target of emulation, fierce jealousy. A few years ago, the term Incel was coined and vaulted into the public consciousness. It means "involuntarily celibate." I read a column about this in which a person argued that society needs to "equally spread around the fruits of the sexual revolution." In case you are not grasping what this demented person was arguing, he was arguing that everybody ought to have access to whomever they want to have sex with, whether that other person is okay with it or not. It is emulation, fierce jealousy. And it is a work of the flesh.

The tenth item on the list is **wrath**. It is from the word *thumos*, and it means hot, ungoverned anger. That also is clearly evident most everywhere in our day. Every day there is some road rage shooting. Almost every day in Chicago, multiple people are murdered in anger. Almost every day brings a new video of kids ganging up on and beating other kids, including the one from today (February 3, 2023) where two fairly sizable kids on the bus, one of them fifteen years old, beat a little nine-year-old girl into the ground. It is wrath, ungoverned anger, and it is a work of the flesh.

The eleventh item on the list is **strife**. It is from the word *eritheia*, and is a very interesting word that means electioneering, intriguing for office, pushing oneself forward. In our vernacular, we would say that it is manipulating things behind-the-scenes for personal advancement.

This happens everywhere. It happens in churches, it happens in schools, it happens at work, it happens in families, it happens in friend groups. Any time someone is manipulating things behind-the-scenes for their own personal advancement, it is strife, and it is a work of the flesh.

The twelfth item on the list is **seditions**. It is from the word *dikostasia*, and it means causing divisions and dissension. It happens in churches when people intentionally try to split and destroy them. It happens in marriages when someone tries to split up a man and wife. It happens in businesses when someone works to destroy the place that employs them. And it is happening in America with people who slander the founding fathers, insult the Constitution, and proclaim that the very land they are so blessed in is the source of all evil in the world.

It is sedition, and it is a work of the flesh.

The thirteenth item on the list is **heresies**. It is from the word *haireeses*, and it is another very interesting word. It means to follow your own beliefs instead of God's beliefs and to capture others in your error. Jamieson, Fausset, and Brown says that it is "a schism that has become inveterate." (394)

Every cult falls under this heading. When people teach things directly contrary to the Word of God, not just a small error born out of misunderstanding a text, but huge, grievous errors on the very fundamental doctrines of the faith, things that will send people to hell if they fall for them, they are heretics, they are teaching heresy. And heresy is a work of the flesh.

The fourteenth item on the list is **envyings**. It is from the word *phthonos*, and, like hatred, it is self-defining. Envy, being resentful of what others have, is everywhere these days. It used to be regarded as one of the worst of sins, but now it is actually fashionable. Socialism is all about envy. Marxism is all about envy. The push to have everyone end up equal no matter the vastly different efforts they put into life is envy.

Several public schools made the news recently because they did not give out honors awards that had been earned, and they tried to hide the fact that those honors had been earned. The reason they did so was because they did not want students who had not earned honors to feel bad... (Nomani, 2022)

It is envy, being resentful of what others have. And it is a work of the flesh.

The fifteenth item on the list is **murders**. It is from the word *phonos*, and it is also very much self-defining. Murder is killing an innocent person.

That is obviously a pretty big one in our day, although it has been going on since the time of Cain. The abortion "doctor" is a murderer. The fentanyl producer is a murderer. The gang banger in Chicago gunning people down in the streets is a murderer. All of these murderers, and all other murderers, should be tried in a court of law and, at minimum, locked away forever. Murder is a work of the flesh.

The sixteenth item on the list is **drunkenness**. It is from the word *methay*, and it means intoxication, drunkenness. This is another one of those sins that is entirely socially acceptable now. But God put it in the same list as murder and adultery and said that it is a work of the flesh.

The seventeenth item on the list is **revellings**. It is from the word *komos*, and it means partying and drunken carousing.

Again, that is so acceptable to society today. Even in so-called Christian circles, this just gets a wink and a nudge. But party boys and party girls are not okay in God's sight. Reveling is a work of the flesh.

Having given those list of seventeen sins, seventeen works of the flesh, Paul then gave this addendum:

"And such like."

In other words, this list does not exhaust the works of the flesh. No list could ever exhaust the works of the flesh since "flesh" in every generation comes up with new and creative ways to express its wickedness. And this tells us that we do not look to Scripture just for a checklist of what is right and what is wrong; we look to Scripture to find principles by which we can evaluate everything as right or wrong.

Two thousand years ago, there was no such thing as doxxing because there was no such thing as the Internet. But the principles we learn from Scripture cover that quite nicely.

Two thousand years ago, there was no such thing as Swatting because there were no such things as SWAT teams. But the principles we learn from Scripture cover that quite nicely.

So pay attention to these very specific seventeen works of the flesh, but pay attention as well to all of the "and such like" that principles of Scripture very clearly deem to be wrong.

Having given this list and having added the *"and such like,"* Paul then gave the conclusion that everyone should pay attention to:

"Of the which I tell you before, as I have also told you in time past, that they which do such things shall not inherit the kingdom of God."

This is one of the reasons why I call this passage *Examine Your Orchard.* Your life will produce a product. It will either produce the works of the flesh or the fruit of the Spirit. If your life is marked by the fruit of the Spirit, you have good reason to claim to be saved. But if your life is marked by any of the works of the flesh, you have no good reason to claim to be saved.

"But I said a prayer when I was little!"

If your life is marked by any of the works of the flesh, you have no good reason to claim to be saved.

"But I saw a vision, and God told me he was with me!"

If your life is marked by any of the works of the flesh, you have no good reason to claim to be saved.

"But I'm filled with the Holy Ghost and speak in tongues!"

If your life is marked by any of the works of the flesh, you have no good reason to claim to be saved.

"But I got baptized!"

If your life is marked by any of the works of the flesh, you have no good reason to claim to be saved.

American Christianity has gotten into a very bad situation, one in which a whole lot of people claim to be saved for one reason or another, and yet, their lives bear no evidence of the fruit of the Spirit and are marked by the works of the flesh.

Look at what Jesus said:

Matthew 7:20 *Wherefore by their fruits ye shall know them.* **21** *Not every one that saith unto me, Lord, Lord, shall enter into the kingdom of heaven; but he that doeth the will of my Father which is in heaven.* **22** *Many will say to me in that day, Lord, Lord, have we not prophesied in thy name? and in thy name have cast out devils? and in thy name done many wonderful works?* **23** *And then will I profess unto them, **I never knew you: depart from me, ye that work iniquity**.*

There are going to be multitudes of people to stand before Christ, absolutely shocked to find out that they do not get to go to heaven. They have religious experiences that they are pointing back to, but they have ignored that their lives are marked by iniquity.

If your life is marked by the fruit of the Spirit, you have good reason to believe that you are saved. But if your life is marked by the works of the flesh, you have no good reason whatsoever to believe that you are saved.

The fruit of the Spirit

Having dealt with a list of seventeen specific individual works of the flesh, Paul will now turn his attention to the conglomerate fruit of the spirit.

Galatians 5:22 *But the fruit of the Spirit is love, joy, peace, longsuffering, gentleness, goodness, faith,* **23** *Meekness, temperance: against such there is no law.*

Once again, please note that this is not fruits, plural, but fruit, singular. All of the works of the flesh may not be manifest in a lost person, but all of the fruit of the Spirit, all nine items that make up the one fruit, will be being produced in a saved person. It is not a buffet of fruits, it is a conglomerate of fruit, and all will be present to one degree or another in everyone who is saved. The degree to which they are present, though, will be in proportion to how much we allow the Spirit to have control in our lives.

So what is on this list that makes up the fruit of the Spirit?

The first part of the fruit is **love**. It comes from the rather famous word *agapay*, and when you examine all that Scripture has to say about it, you arrive at a definition that goes something like this: a self-sacrificial giving of one's self for others.

Here are some verses that use that word and that demonstrate that definition:

John 15:13 *Greater love hath no man than this, that a man lay down his life for his friends.*

John 3:16 *For God so loved the world, that he gave his only begotten Son, that whosoever believeth in him should not perish, but have everlasting life.*

Romans 5:8 *But God commendeth his love toward us, in that, while we were yet sinners, Christ died for us.*

Love, real love, love produced in us by the Holy Spirit, will always think of the highest benefit to others rather than oneself. This is why it is so ridiculous to ascribe the word "love" to things that are harmful to others, things like homosexuality, adultery, and premarital sex. What it boils down to is that the world calls lust love, when real love is willing to set aside one's deepest desires for the good of another. Whenever someone engages in activity with another, activity that does spiritual and emotional and even incredible physical harm, as with the case of homosexuality, it is never love. In many cases, I am quite certain that people think it is love, but that is because they do not understand the definition of real love.

Another obvious application of this is the fact that Christians are accused of not loving sinners when it is really non-Christians or very weak and carnal Christians who are guilty of not loving sinners. Real love does what is best for others. And the best thing for sinners is to be confronted with their sin so that they can be saved and avoid having to go to hell.

There is currently a video circulating of a rather famous mega-church preacher preaching his latest bit of heresy. In this particular clip, he discusses homosexuality. He acknowledges that several Bible passages speak against it, and then he simply waives those passages off as, in his words, "clobber passages," and proceeds to tell us how wonderful these people are and how the church needs to embrace them and take them in and treat them like brothers and sisters in Christ.

He is sending people to hell and calling it love.

Real love is the doctor telling you about your cancer, even if you do not want to hear it, and offering a solution if he can.

Real love is the officer knocking on your door in the middle of the night to tell you that someone you love has been

153

in a wreck, knowing that the next thing he is going to hear is wailing and screaming.

Real love is the child of God who looks a sinner in the eyes and says, "What you are doing is sin, and you need to repent and be saved."

This also plays out in the obvious application, marriage and the home. Real love is when someone gets paralyzed or debilitated, and the other continues to stay and care for them. Real love is when things are hard in the home and marriage, and rather than bail out, people stay and work through it.

Real love always thinks of the highest benefit of others before oneself. And this is not natural to us. This is not a work of the flesh. The flesh tells us, "Look out for number one!" It is the Spirit that produces His fruit in our life that says, "You are called to love that person, so put them before yourself."

The second part of the fruit is **joy**. It comes from the word *cara*, and it means brightness, specifically a brightness of attitude. A true child of God will not be a Dark Donny or Gloomy Gloria. Things may not always be good; there will be some hard days, but there will also be a Spirit-produced brightness about them.

Do believers often get very down? Certainly. Elijah did. Jeremiah did. John the Baptist did. But those hard times are actually when we most need to discipline ourselves to focus on and seek out this fruit. Look at what Jesus said to His disciples in one of their darkest moments, the time when He was heading for Gethsemane to be taken and to suffer and to die:

John 15:11 *These things have I spoken unto you, that my joy might remain in you, and that your joy might be full.*

Joy, for the Spirit-filled believer, is not dependent on circumstances. It comes from within, not from without. It makes our grief more bearable; it helps us to keep on going and living when others would give up; it makes the sun shine again far

154

faster than it does for the despondent, lost soul who has no hope. And it is part of the fruit of the Spirit.

The third part of the fruit is **peace**. It is from the word *eiraynay*, and it means calmness, tranquility, and assurance. I could spend many hours and write many volumes just on this one word, this one part of the fruit; nothing is so craved and yet so lacking in people today as peace! And the main reason it is lacking is because people do not even know the source of it. They are like people drilling into the air, hoping to strike the oil that is only found deep underground.

Peace, real peace, is the fruit of the Spirit. It is produced in the heart and mind and life of a believer who is allowing the Holy Spirit to have control. Jesus, during the very same walk to Gethsemane that I wrote of a moment ago, also spoke of peace to His troubled men:

John 14:27 *Peace I leave with you, my peace I give unto you: not as the world giveth, give I unto you. Let not your heart be troubled, neither let it be afraid.*

When we are filled with the Spirit, He produces a peace in us that transcends our circumstances. That does not mean we will never get scared; the Paul who wrote this often did. But peace always followed the fear until one day, he was even able to say, *"For I am now ready to be offered, and the time of my departure is at hand."* (**2 Timothy 4:6**).

When you, as a child of God, can speak that calmly about your coming execution, it is the fruit of the Spirit; it is peace.

The fourth part of the fruit is **longsuffering**. It is from the word *makrothumia*. It means being patient with others since God has been patient with us. Adam Clarke put it this way "[Longsuffering means] long-mindedness, bearing with the frailties and provocations of others, from the consideration that God has borne long with ours; and that, if he had not, we should have been speedily consumed: bearing up also through all the troubles and difficulties of life without murmuring or repining;

155

submitting cheerfully to every dispensation of God's providence, and thus deriving benefit from every occurrence." (413)

If there is ever anything that is not natural, this is it. It is not natural to calmly smile and ignore it when someone in traffic salutes you with just one finger. It is not natural to calmly smile and ignore it when someone cuts in line in front of you. It is not natural to calmly smile and ignore it when someone uses a slur on you. It is not natural to calmly smile and ignore it when someone screams at you. It is not natural to calmly smile and ignore it when someone leaves something laying on the floor or plays "Mount Platemore" with the dishes in the sink.

There are infinite numbers of possible things that we face each day at work, at school, at home, and definitely online that make us want to clap back in anger and harshness. That is a natural response. But the fruit of the Spirit is longsuffering, being patient with others since God has been patient with us.

If you and I are going to diligently pray for anything on this list to be produced in us in greater abundance, it should probably be this.

The fifth part of the fruit is **gentleness**. It is from the word *kraystotays,* and it means kindness, benignity, or, to put it in practical terms, it means not being hard, cold, and mean, being easy to be around.

This, like the one before it, is not really a natural thing. It is more natural in some than in others, but it is really not totally natural in any of us. Adam Clarke had a very understated comment on this, saying that gentleness is "a very rare grace, often wanting in many who have a considerable share of Christian excellence." (413)

He is correct. Even among many Christians who do fine in many other areas, this particular part of the fruit of the Spirit is often sorely lacking.

I have pretty well lost count of the caustic Christians I have met through the years, both in the pulpit and in the pews.

Many, many, many times, I have been really kind to people, only to have them, out of the blue, spew horrible hatred and venom at me. They lack gentleness.

Many, many, many times, I have sat in a meeting and listened to well-respected preachers get downright vulgar and coarse as they swung the sword at "enemies" who weren't really even enemies. They lack gentleness.

Almost daily, I see believers online being absolutely hateful to people, even other believers. Mind you, contending for the faith is a command (Jude 1:3). But being a hateful jerk is not. Truth all by itself is offensive and divisive; there is no need to add human hatefulness on top of that.

Believers ought to cultivate this particular part of the fruit of the Spirit, gentleness. We should not be hard, cold, and mean; we should be easy to be around.

Let me tell you a "full circle" story. When I was about sixteen, I went to a huge youth rally. The pastor of that church was the preacher that night. I was in awe of him when I walked in; the place was huge, and 1,500 people were packed in. And all during the message, he was hateful. And when I went to shake his hand and speak to him at the door afterward, he was just as hateful. Not just to me but to our entire youth group. I was blown away; I was not expecting that at all.

I never forgot it. And then, a few years ago, I was asked to come preach at their school. The pastor was long since gone, and a new pastor, a very good man, had taken his place. I stood and preached in the very pulpit that hateful preacher preached to me from. And afterward, I hung around long enough to greet each kid and say a kind word to them. And recently, I preached there again and, by request, went and worked out with some of their guys. I took some time to teach them what I knew. I got to know them. I will likely never be as famous as the first guy, but if I can be gentle, if I can be easy to be around, that is better. It is better because gentleness is part of the fruit of the Spirit.

The sixth part of the fruit is **goodness**. It is from the word *agathosunay,* and it means uprightness of heart, doing that which is good. Barnes put it this way, "Here the word seems to be used in the sense of beneficence, or a disposition to do good to others. The sense is, that a Christian must be a good man." (Lindner)

One of our men, when we were starting our homeless ministry, disguised himself as a homeless man and went and lived on the streets of Gastonia for a few days to see what it was like for them, so he would best know how to help them. That is goodness, and it is part of the fruit of the Spirit.

A girl being raised by a drunk single father came to our church years ago and wore the same tattered, stained dress three weeks in a row. It was clear she had no idea how to take care of herself or her clothes. So without being asked, some of our teenage girls went and picked her up one day and took her out for a "girls' day." Using their own money, they bought her a bunch of new clothes, got her hair styled and her nails done, and she came in the next Sunday with the bearing and confidence of a princess. That is goodness, and it is part of the fruit of the Spirit.

Some kids we brought on the bus had their apartment burn down the week before Christmas. Within twenty-four hours, our church had completely packed our six-by-ten-foot church trailer with new stuff, twice, and taken it over to them. That is goodness, and it is part of the fruit of the Spirit.

One of our church families fell on some hard times; all of their vehicles fell apart, and they could not even get to work. Another of our families brought their own personal vehicle over to them, with the title, and simply gave it to them. That is goodness, and it is part of the fruit of the Spirit.

The seventh part of the fruit is **faith**. It is from the word *pistis,* and it means a couple of different things, trusting and believing God in every aspect of life and being faithful to the truth and to God's service. It encompasses both what we believe and how we behave.

We are to trust God in everything, and we are to be able to be trusted by God in everything. When He sees us, He should see people that have confidence in Him and people that He can have confidence in.

Most of our Christian circle is praying for the family of a man who had been proclaimed dead but is now very much alive. It may take him years to recover, but he is getting a little better each day. His wife had absolute faith in God when she thought her husband was dying, and when she thought he was dead, and now that she knows he is alive but has so very far to go to recover. And she herself has been faithful to God and to serve God by serving her husband and kids through it all.

It is faith, and it is part of the fruit of the Spirit.

The eighth part of the fruit is **meekness**. It is from the word *prayotays,* and Adam Clarke defines it well when he says that it is "Mildness, indulgence toward the weak and erring, patient suffering of injuries without feeling a spirit of revenge, an even balance of all tempers and passions, the entire opposite to anger." (413)

Mind you, it does not at all mean weakness, as scoffers often view it. Moses was described as *"very meek, above all the men which were upon the face of the earth"* (**Numbers 12:3**). And yet there was absolutely nothing weak about him. He killed a man with his bare hands for assaulting a fellow Hebrew; he faced off against multiple jerks who were bullying the daughters of the priest of Midian; he ground the golden calf to powder and made everybody drink it; he was a man's man!

And yet he was also the meekest man on earth. His strength was fully under control, he was level-headed, and he was patient. It is meekness, and it is part of the fruit of the Spirit.

The ninth part of the fruit is **temperance**. It is from the word *egkrateia,* and it means self-control, the mastering of fleshly passions.

If there has ever been something lacking in most all of the lost world and also in a great deal of Christianity, this is it. Not only is it lacking, it is not even regarded as a good thing anymore. The mantra of our day is, "Live your life your way; make yourself happy; you deserve whatever you want whenever you want it." The idea of telling yourself "no" when it comes to things you want is regarded as a relic of a bygone, Victorian era.

But God still expects temperance from us, and the Holy Spirit still works to produce it in us.

Do you want to drink booze? Don't. God expects temperance of us. Do you want to commit adultery? Don't. God expects temperance of us. Do you want to eat like a moose? Don't. God expects temperance of us. Do you want to look at porn? Don't. God expects temperance of us. Do you want to engage in homosexual or lesbian behavior? Don't. God expects temperance of us. Do you want to stay up all night playing video games rather than going to bed so you can be up early enough to read your Bible and get to work on time? Don't. God expects temperance of us.

Look at how Paul put it in another place:

1 Corinthians 9:25 *And every man that striveth for the mastery is **temperate** in all things. Now they do it to obtain a corruptible crown; but we an incorruptible. 26 I therefore so run, not as uncertainly; so fight I, not as one that beateth the air: 27 But I keep under my body, and bring it into subjection: lest that by any means, when I have preached to others, I myself should be a castaway.*

Paul "*kept his body under,*" meaning he actively denied it much of what it wanted. Our overeating, sexually indulgent, perverted, lazy, self-entitled generation knows nothing of temperance. And yet it is essential; it is part of the fruit of the Spirit.

These are the things that God absolutely will be producing in the life of a saved person. Again, the degree to which He does so will be in proportion to how much we allow the Spirit to have control in our lives, but this fruit absolutely will be being produced in us if we are truly saved.

In observing this list, Paul said, *"against such there is no law."* In one form or another, in one place or another, there is a law against all of the works of the flesh. But there is no law against the fruit of the Spirit. These are things that even the lost world respects!

The choice of our walk

Galatians 5:24 *And they that are Christ's have crucified the flesh with the affections and lusts.*

Whoever is a born-again child of God is a person who is not under the power of the works of the flesh. When you get saved, your old man is crucified with Christ, by choice. When the lost sinner comes asking for salvation, if he truly means it, he comes with the understanding that he is bad, his behavior is bad, and Christ will not allow it to be left that way. He comes repenting of sin. He crucifies his flesh by handing it to Christ, who became our sin and died on the cross. That old flesh dies, and the believing sinner becomes an entirely new creature in Christ (2 Corinthians 5:17).

So if a saved person sins after that, it is not because they have to; it is because they choose to. A lost person *has* to sin in one way or another, but a saved person *chooses* to sin.

Galatians 5:25 *If we live in the Spirit, let us also walk in the Spirit.*

If we live in the Spirit means "If we have been made alive by the Spirit, if we are saved." So if we are saved, we need to walk like we are saved. Our position is secure; our practice needs attending to.

Galatians 5:26 *Let us not be desirous of vain glory, provoking one another, envying one another.*

It is interesting that Paul put this right at the end of these two lists. Why would he do that? Because whoever walks after the works of the flesh will not just be fighting with God but also with people. Whoever has the fruit of the Spirit being produced in his life will not just get along with God but with people as well.

After pointing out that the flesh produces a list of bad works, and the Holy Spirit produces a list of good works, why would it be necessary for Paul to warn us to walk after the Spirit and not after the flesh? Because we are still a saved soul in a lost body. There will still be a battle to face. Even though the saved person absolutely will have the fruit of the Spirit in his or her life, it will still be possible for him to slip and sin in the works of the flesh. It will not be possible for him to live a life that is characterized by those works, though. If you can look at somebody and say, "They *got* drunk," maybe they are a backslidden Christian. But if you can look at somebody and truthfully say, "They *are* habitually a drunk," then they are lost. If you can look at somebody and say, "They committed adultery," maybe they are a backslidden Christian. But if you can look at somebody and truthfully say, "They *are* a habitual adulterer or adulteress," then they are lost.

No matter what the sin, if a person can live in it as a lifestyle without being under awful conviction and experiencing terrible chastisement that either cures them or kills them, they are just plain lost.

So, Examine Your Orchard!

Chapter Thirteen
Family Matters

Galatians 6:1 *Brethren, if a man be overtaken in a fault, ye which are spiritual, restore such an one in the spirit of meekness; considering thyself, lest thou also be tempted.* **2** *Bear ye one another's burdens, and so fulfil the law of Christ.* **3** *For if a man think himself to be something, when he is nothing, he deceiveth himself.* **4** *But let every man prove his own work, and then shall he have rejoicing in himself alone, and not in another.* **5** *For every man shall bear his own burden.* **6** *Let him that is taught in the word communicate unto him that teacheth in all good things.* **7** *Be not deceived; God is not mocked: for whatsoever a man soweth, that shall he also reap.* **8** *For he that soweth to his flesh shall of the flesh reap corruption; but he that soweth to the Spirit shall of the Spirit reap life everlasting.* **9** *And let us not be weary in well doing: for in due season we shall reap, if we faint not.* **10** *As we have therefore opportunity, let us do good unto all men, especially unto them who are of the household of faith.*

As Paul so often did, as he got to the end of his letter, he got very practical and personal. He truly loved these people and wanted to help them. So in the verses we will be examining, you will notice that Paul was dealing with several important matters for the household of faith.

163

Matters of sin and restoration

Galatians 6:1 *Brethren, if a man be overtaken in a fault, ye which are spiritual, restore such an one in the spirit of meekness; considering thyself, lest thou also be tempted.*

There is a lot here in just a few words, and it is incredibly valuable to us. Note first of all that Paul is dealing with "brethren." He is writing *to* people who are saved, *about* people who are saved. And what he writes here is very similar to what he wrote to the Corinthian church in his second letter to them. In that instance, a man had sinned grievously, Paul had instructed them to remove him from among them, and they did. But when he repented, they continued to shun him. So Paul had to write back to them telling them to restore the repentant believer!

Paul spoke here in our text of the fact that a person could be *"overtaken in a fault."* That phrase means to "fall into sin without pre-meditation," to "be surprised by wickedness:" Albert Barnes put it this way:

"It is a case which the apostle supposes might happen, Christians were not perfect; and it was possible that they who were true Christians might be surprised by temptation, and fall into sin." (Lindner)

He went on to say:

"The doctrine taught by Paul is, that such is human infirmity, and such the strength of human depravity, that no one knows into what sins he may himself fall. He may be tempted to commit the same sins which he endeavours to amend in others; he may be left to commit even worse sins. If this is the case, we should be tender, while we are firm; forgiving, while we set our faces against evil; prayerful, while we rebuke; and compassionate, when we are compelled to inflict on others the discipline of the church. Every man who has any proper feelings, when he attempts to recover an erring brother, should pray for him and for himself also; and will regard his duty as only half done, and that very imperfectly, if he does not 'consider also that he himself may be tempted.' " (Lindner)

In Galatians, that very thing had happened. People who had no intentions of disobeying God were taken off guard by the Judaizers, surprised by their smooth attack, and had fallen into error.

How many of you, dear readers, would be so kind as to admit that this has happened to you at some point? Anyone who is honest would have to put themselves in this number. We are still in bodies of flesh, so at some point, we will all slip and fall, whether it be into doctrinal fault or behavioral fault. We are flesh. We can sin, and we can also be stupid. And when a brother or sister in Christ slips and falls, there are some predictable ways that people will react.

Some will be haughty, saying, "I knew it was only a matter of time."

Some will be proud, happy that they are so much purer than those backsliders are.

Many will be harsh, wanting to drop the hammer of judgment immediately.

But Paul did not label any of those things as spiritual. If you are spiritual, when a person slips and falls (not when they openly defy God and live in sin, that is another story), our task is that of restoration. And that word for "restore" should teach us something: It means "to bring back into place like you would a dislocated limb." (Clarke, 414)

When a person dislocates an arm, they want a medical person to carefully and gently put that member of their body back into place. But unfortunately, when a member of the body of Christ slips and falls, many people want to amputate that limb! Paul said, "No, restore it."

There are so many ways that people pendulum swing away from what God wants. Some will take a libertine attitude towards fault and "just let things be."

Others take an executioner's attitude toward sin and try to destroy anyone who falls into fault.

But Paul said, "If they slip, restore them!" Have you ever needed restoring? If a person needs it, and is willing to have it, we ought to be in the restoration business as far as we are able to do so. Mind you, some things can bring issues that can never be fully rectified, and some offices and positions can be forfeit forever by a single action, but the fullest restoration still possible is always to be our goal when dealing with a fallen brother or sister.

And look again at the attitude that is to accompany this:

...ye which are spiritual, restore such an one in the spirit of meekness;

The spiritual person is not the one who looks down his or her nose at whoever slipped and fell. The spiritual one is the one who can be meek, humble, Christ-like, and restore a person.

Haughty and spiritual are on opposite ends of the spectrum; you cannot be both haughty and spiritual. And here is some excellent motivation for doing right in this. If you are proud, haughty, if you think you are better than whoever has fallen, look at what Paul gives as motivation for meekness:

...considering thyself, lest thou also be tempted.

In other words, do not be too hard on whoever has fallen; you could very well be next!

I could write true example after example of this. I could tell you about a great many parents who have looked down long, pious noses at other people's kids who did wrong, only to have theirs be next.

166

I have also seen quite a few preachers smirk at the fall of other preachers, only to be next month's sermon illustration.

I have seen more than one couple talk arrogantly of the marital problems of others, only to find themselves sitting across from my desk not too long after.

Whatever someone has fallen into, if they are sorry and repentant, do not be too hard on them because you may be the next one in need of mercy.

Matters of support and responsibility

Galatians 6:2 *Bear ye one another's burdens, and so fulfil the law of Christ.*

Before we get too deeply into this verse, let me show you verse five and teach you something so that you do not come to the flawed conclusion that there is a contradiction in Scripture:

Galatians 6:5 *For every man shall bear his own burden.*

Verse two says, "*Bear ye one another's burdens,*" but verse five says, "*every man shall bear his own burden.*" Is that a contradiction in Scripture? No. These two verses are talking about two completely different things. The word for burden in verse two is *baray*, and it means "a weight." The word for burden in verse five is a completely different word, the word *fortion*, and it was a shipping term which meant "a bill of lading," an "invoice for the cargo." Hold that thought as we go through these verses.

In verse two, based on the definition we just saw, Paul told us to fulfill the law of Christ by helping to bear the burdens, carry the weight, of our brothers and sisters in Christ. The context beginning in verse one lets us know that the primary thing Paul had in mind was the restoration of an erring brother. There are things that any of us could fall into, "burdens" in the form of temptations that may ensnare us. Helping one another to avoid those snares and helping to restore those who have so fallen is the least we can do and the best way that we can help one another with those burdens.

But this truth obviously applies in a much wider sense as well. Any way that we can help to bear the burdens, the heavy loads of others, is also the least we can do. Matthew Henry also recognized those two different things as truths that can be rightly drawn from this verse, saying,

> "This may be considered either as referring to what goes before, and so may teach us to exercise forbearance and compassion towards one another, in the case of those weaknesses, and follies, and infirmities, which too often attend us—that, though we should not wholly connive at them, yet we should not be severe against one another on account of them; or as a more general precept, and so it directs us to sympathize with one another under the various trials and troubles that we may meet with, and to be ready to afford each other the comfort and counsel, the help and assistance, which our circumstances may require." (Henry, 679)

When you know of a financial need of a burdened brother or sister in Christ and help meet it, you are obeying this verse.

When you see something that needs fixed for someone, and you do it, you are obeying this verse.

When you sit in the waiting room of a hospital with people, you are obeying this verse.

Many Christians want to be fruit inspectors, but far fewer want to be burden bearers!

Galatians 6:3 *For if a man think himself to be something, when he is nothing, he deceiveth himself.*

Take this verse in context. If you are not obeying verse two, especially when it comes to helping in the restoration of a fallen brother, then you may think you are something, but you are nothing! You have fooled yourself.

Galatians 6:4 *But let every man prove his own work, and then shall he have rejoicing in himself alone, and not in another.*

Paul is still on the same topic. And in this topic, he now uses the interesting word "prove," which is from the word *dokimadzo.* It means to "put to the test." In context, he is saying, "Let every man see whether he is helping to bear other's burdens, and whether or not he is as prone to fall as the one whom he has seen fall. Let him prove, test himself in those regards. Let him be more diligent to judge himself than others; let him be more critical of his own potential weaknesses than any that he deems himself better than."

If a person does that, he can rejoice in what God is doing through him rather than having to find someone "not as good" to compare himself with so he can pat himself on the back. If we have to find others worse than ourselves to give us something to rejoice in, then there is not much of worth to us at all!

Galatians 6:5 *For every man shall bear his own burden.*

Do you remember that word for "burden" in this verse, *fortion*, "a bill of lading," an "invoice for the cargo?" This is where that definition gets pretty important. Just one verse earlier, we learned that we should live our life in such a way that we can rejoice over it without having to compare ourselves to others. Now we learn that this distinction will follow us to the very Judgment Seat of Christ. Every child of God will answer for himself or herself there; no comparisons will be allowed!

If you were planning on bringing a list of people that you were better than to that meeting, rethink that plan. God will allow no comparisons on that day; every one of us will answer for ourselves to God as if we were the only people on earth all the time we lived our lives.

Galatians 6:6 *Let him that is taught in the word communicate unto him that teacheth in all good things.*

169

In verse six, the subject segues into another section on the same topic. Paul used this subject, helping one another, to turn the Galatian church's attention to their care of the man of God because his burdens were worthy of bearing just as much as anyone else's.

He said to *communicate to him that teacheth in all good things*! In other words, take care of him financially, look for physical needs that you can meet, find areas and ways to be a blessing to him. Robert Jamieson put it this way when explaining this verse, "From the mention of bearing one another's burdens, he passes to one way in which those burdens may be borne—by ministering out of their earthly goods to their spiritual teachers." (Jamieson)

In a lot of churches, this does not happen. I thank God and am very grateful that in mine, it does. A church ought to examine a pastor's vehicle situation, food situation, insurance situation, salary situation, housing situation, whatever situation, and find a way to take proper care of him. I love the way Adam Clarke put this way back in the early eighteen hundreds:

"Contribute to the support of the man who has dedicated himself to the work of the ministry, and who gives up his time and his life to preach the Gospel. It appears that some of the believers in Galatia could receive the Christian ministry without contributing to its support. This is both ungrateful and base. We do not expect that a common schoolmaster will give up his time to teach our children their alphabet without being paid for it; and can we suppose that it is just for any person to sit under the preaching of the Gospel in order to grow wise unto salvation by it, and not contribute to the support of the spiritual teacher? It is unjust." (415)

This was a theme, by the way, that Paul broached many more times than just here to the Galatians:

1 Corinthians 9:3 *Mine answer to them that do examine me is this,* **4** *Have we not power to eat and to drink?* **5** *Have we*

170

not power to lead about a sister, a wife, as well as other apostles, and as the brethren of the Lord, and Cephas? **6** *Or I only and Barnabas, have not we power to forbear working?* **7** *Who goeth a warfare any time at his own charges? who planteth a vineyard, and eateth not of the fruit thereof? or who feedeth a flock, and eateth not of the milk of the flock?* **8** *Say I these things as a man? or saith not the law the same also?* **9** *For it is written in the law of Moses, Thou shalt not muzzle the mouth of the ox that treadeth out the corn. Doth God take care for oxen?* **10** *Or saith he it altogether for our sakes? For our sakes, no doubt, this is written: that he that ploweth should plow in hope; and that he that thresheth in hope should be partaker of his hope.* **11** *If we have sown unto you spiritual things, is it a great thing if we shall reap your carnal things?*

That whole passage was about properly paying the man of God, not expecting him to work a full-time secular job and then add a free full-time ministerial load on top of that.

Here is how he put it to Timothy:

1 Timothy 5:17 *Let the elders that rule well be counted worthy of double honour, especially they who labour in the word and doctrine.*

We get our word "honorarium" from the word honor. It is from the word *timay,* and it means a fixed value.

As a person who travels all over the place preaching, my estimation is that for every one prosperity pimp preacher who is living a lavish lifestyle, there are a thousand good preachers who would starve to death if it were up to the people they give their lives and greatest efforts for.

From the pulpit to the pew, we should do everything in our power to take care of each other.

Matters of sowing and reaping

Galatians 6:7 *Be not deceived; God is not mocked: for whatsoever a man soweth, that shall he also reap.* **8** *For he that* *soweth to his flesh shall of the flesh reap corruption; but he that soweth to the Spirit shall of the Spirit reap life everlasting.*

Now we find another slight segue, while once again still in the same general topic. Paul has been talking about restoring each other, taking care of each other, and taking care of God's man. And now he moves smoothly into the larger subject of sowing and reaping out of that narrow focus on specific sowing and reaping. And in so doing, he gave us some of the greatest, most practical verses in the Bible. Again, they describe the law of sowing and reaping and teach us that we will not sin and get by, nor will we do right and go unrewarded!

Even Christians can "sow to their flesh." They can backslide, they can be overtaken in a fault and then stay there, but there will always, always, always be consequences!

There are consequences for fornication, and drinking, and smoking, and doing drugs, and for everything that is wrong or ill-advised or both. Live right because it is right, but also because it is beneficial! Only an idiot ignores the fact that it pays to do right. If you do wrong in this life, then in this life you will experience the trouble that it causes. If you do right in this life, then in this life you will begin to experience the benefits of life everlasting. Jesus put it this way:

John 10:10 *The thief cometh not, but for to steal, and to kill, and to destroy: I am come that they might have life, and that they might have it more abundantly.*

I do not just want "life"; I want *abundant* life! All of us should want that. We should all want to live our lives in such a way that our heavenly Father wants to bless us as the Son promised us.

Galatians 6:9 *And let us not be weary in well doing: for in due season we shall reap, if we faint not.*

The reason for this verse is pretty apparent. Paul just got done telling us about the law of sowing and reaping, which is not just a negative truth, but also a positive truth. But the benefits of living right do not always show up immediately. In fact, sometimes it takes years. This verse, then, is designed as an encouragement for us to keep doing right. We may not "reap immediately," but we will reap if we keep doing right and faint not.

This is true in regard to purity, the ministry, marriage, hard work, anything that is good!

Galatians 6:10 *As we have therefore opportunity, let us do good unto all men, especially unto them who are of the household of faith.*

The subject has still not changed; we see that from the word "therefore." So this also applies to sowing and reaping. And do you see that, though we are to do good to all men in general, we are to focus most on doing good to the household of faith? This is the saved, the church, those you worship with and serve with each week.

We should not mind helping the outside world when we can, but our emphasis is to be on helping our brothers and sisters in Christ! Why? Because we are family, and these are just simple obvious Family Matters.

Chapter Fourteen
One Thing to Shout About

Galatians 6:11 *Ye see how large a letter I have written unto you with mine own hand. 12 As many as desire to make a fair shew in the flesh, they constrain you to be circumcised; only lest they should suffer persecution for the cross of Christ. 13 For neither they themselves who are circumcised keep the law; but desire to have you circumcised, that they may glory in your flesh. 14 But God forbid that I should glory, save in the cross of our Lord Jesus Christ, by whom the world is crucified unto me, and I unto the world. 15 For in Christ Jesus neither circumcision availeth any thing, nor uncircumcision, but a new creature. 16 And as many as walk according to this rule, peace be on them, and mercy, and upon the Israel of God. 17 From henceforth let no man trouble me: for I bear in my body the marks of the Lord Jesus. 18 Brethren, the grace of our Lord Jesus Christ be with your spirit. Amen.*

When it all came down to it, when Paul had dealt so thoroughly with the errors of the Judaizers, when he had shown that all the things that they were shouting about were worthless, Paul himself gave the Galatians the one thing that there really is to shout about. Jesus Christ hung on an old rugged cross, endured the pain, reached down to grab man and up to reach

God, and paid the debt for our sins. That dear reader, is something to shout about.

These last eight verses are Paul's closing remarks to the people he loved in Galatia. As personal as they are, I am not going to restrict these verses by forcing them into an outline. We will just take them verse by verse, and soak in what is there.

Galatians 6:11 *Ye see how large a letter I have written unto you with mine own hand.*

Let me tell you first of all what this does not mean. It is not talking about how long the book of Galatians is, because it is not a long book. Galatians only has six chapters. By comparison, Romans has sixteen, 1 Corinthians has sixteen, and 2 Corinthians has thirteen.

When he spoke of this being a large letter, he was talking about the size of his writing. Remember that in chapter four verse fifteen, we learned that Paul had poor eyesight. Many of the letters he wrote, he dictated to an amanuensis, a scribe. This one he actually wrote, and he had to write it big just to see what he was writing.

Why did he mention this? Remember that the Judaizers had been claiming that Paul said a lot of things that he did not really say. He did not want them to successfully dispute that he actually wrote this letter, so he pointed out what would be a solid proof to those Galatians who knew him.

Galatians 6:12 *As many as desire to make a fair shew in the flesh, they constrain you to be circumcised; only lest they should suffer persecution for the cross of Christ.*

The phrase "*make a fair show in the flesh*" may not be one people use commonly anymore, but I think most everyone can easily understand it. What the Judaizers taught and practiced was not about devotion to God, it was about being acceptable to men. They wanted to look good; they wanted to be liked.

And that is a disaster waiting to happen. The desire to be liked is what leads kids to give up their virginity. The desire to be liked is generally what makes kids start smoking. The desire to be liked is generally what makes people first put booze to their lips. The desire to be liked is why a huge percentage of high school kids now call themselves non-binary or trans or LGBTQ or some other such nonsense because it is the shiny new thing that all of the "cool kids" are involved in. The desire to be liked is even what makes people abandon sound doctrine!

In this case, the Judaizers' desire to "*make a fair show in the flesh*" made them insist that the Galatians be circumcised. If they had actually accepted the gospel of grace, they would have ended up being persecuted. Judaism was well-liked and acceptable in the region of Galatia; Christianity was not. The Judaizers did not want to embrace the cross or have any of their proselytes do so. The cross would have cost them too much, in their view. They were giving up eternity to be acceptable to men!

Galatians 6:13 *For neither they themselves who are circumcised keep the law; but desire to have you circumcised, that they may glory in your flesh.*

These Judaizers did not keep "the law;" they kept a few favorite parts of the law. And they were not interested in converting the Galatians, they were just interested in circumcising them. Hauling the Galatians up to the temple and shouting, "Hey, I just won these guys to Christ!" was not going to make anyone pat them on the back. But hauling them up there and saying, "Hey, I just got these guys to be circumcised!" would earn them the accolades of all of the "important people." It was all about glory. And that thought is what led Paul to say this:

Galatians 6:14 *But God forbid that I should glory, save in the cross of our Lord Jesus Christ, by whom the world is crucified unto me, and I unto the world.*

Here is that one thing to shout about. Our rituals are not worth shouting about, our traditions are not worth shouting about, but what Jesus did on Calvary, that is worth shouting

177

about! Paul said, "God forbid" about the idea of glorying in anything but the cross. It is an extremely strident prohibition, a "may it never be" that can only be fully felt in the words "God forbid!"

And did you see what the cross did for Paul? It did not just crucify Jesus. Paul said the cross crucified the world to him and crucified him to the world. That shows the separation that the cross brings. As far as the world was concerned, Paul was as good as dead to them since he got saved. And as far as Paul was concerned, the world was as good as dead to him since he got saved.

When a person truly gets saved, hating sin and staying away from it is not really difficult for them! A person who has seen the value of the cross cannot help but see the worthlessness of the world. Not the souls, mind you; Christ died for those. The word used here is *kosmos*, and means "the arrangement, how things work, the value system." A person who loves that world has never truly come to understand and embrace the cross.

Galatians 6:15 *For in Christ Jesus neither circumcision availeth any thing, nor uncircumcision, but a new creature.*

Nothing racial or religious avails anything before God. The word for availeth is *eskewoh*, and it means to have strength. In other words, things of the flesh have no power to save. Jewish and circumcised avails nothing. Gentile and uncircumcised avails nothing. All God cares about is have you been born again, have you become the new creature in Christ that 2 Corinthians 5:17 speaks of?

Galatians 6:16 *And as many as walk according to this rule, peace be on them, and mercy, and upon the Israel of God.*

The rule that Paul refers to here is the rule that salvation is by faith in Jesus Christ, without any works on our part. But then comes the interesting phrase "and upon the Israel of God."

The Bible speaks of "the Israel of the flesh" in 1 Corinthians 10:18, and "the Israel of God" here. Israel of the flesh is literal Israel, those who are descended from Abraham, Isaac, and Jacob. Israel of God is the saved, those who have been born again of any race including the Jews. Israel of the flesh is still very special to God and has certain promises that He has made them that He will fulfill for them. But Israel of God is even more special to Him, and the promises He has made to us are even better. The Jews will get the Middle East during the Millennial Reign; the saved get heaven for eternity!

Galatians 6:17 *From henceforth let no man trouble me: for I bear in my body the marks of the Lord Jesus.*

This is one of the most personal, raw statements Paul ever made. He lays aside the mantle of apostle and theologian in this verse and bares his back, as it were, showing the price he paid as a human being to bring the gospel to the Galatians and others. And the word he used for marks was *stigmata*, we get our word stigma from it. It represented both physical and emotional wounds. But in this case, Paul was clearly pointing mostly to the physical wounds, things the Galatians could have seen and remembered.

Marks? Oh yes, Paul did indeed have marks in his flesh:

2 Corinthians 11:24 *Of the Jews five times received I forty stripes save one.* **25** *Thrice was I beaten with rods, once was I stoned, thrice I suffered shipwreck, a night and a day I have been in the deep;* **26** *In journeyings often, in perils of waters, in perils of robbers, in perils by mine own countrymen, in perils by the heathen, in perils in the city, in perils in the wilderness, in perils in the sea, in perils among false brethren;* **27** *In weariness and painfulness, in watchings often, in hunger and thirst, in fastings often, in cold and nakedness.*

When Paul resorted to reminding the Galatians that he had been physically abused in order to bring them the gospel, it was his way of reminding the Galatians that they had every reason to listen to him, and no reason to listen to the Judaizers. He had paid a high price for what he did; the Judaizers paid no price at all for their beliefs and practices. Paul said, "From now on, let no man trouble me;" his wounds should have been enough to stop all debate. Those who have, as the old-timers would say, "skin in the game," should be regarded as more trustworthy than those who risk nothing.

Remember this. Never let someone who has not paid the price for the gospel pull you away from someone who has!

Galatians 6:18 *Brethren, the grace of our Lord Jesus Christ be with your spirit. Amen.*

Grace, grace, this whole thing came down to grace. It was grace that saved the Galatians, it was grace that the Judaizers were trying to get them away from, and it was grace that Paul was drawing them back to. There is the yoke of bondage, and there is the grace of God.

There is the slavery of the law and *The Treasures of Liberty.*

Works Cited

Butler, D. R., Ray, A., & Gregory, L. (1995). *America's Dumbest Criminals*. Rutledge Hill Press.

Clarke, A. (1977). *The Holy Bible, Containing the Old and New Testaments, wtih Commentary by Adam Clarke* (Vol. 6). Abingdon-Cokesbury Press.

Difference between messianic judaism and Christianity. Jewish Voice. (2017, March 22). https://www.jewishvoice. org/read/blog/difference-between-messianic-judaism-and-christianity

Editors, R. D. (2022, November 24). *How a man survived a plane crash-and a 15-hour swim with Sharks.* Reader's Digest. https://www.rd.com/article/shark-attack-plane-crash-survivor/

Henry, M. (n.d.). *Matthew Henry's commentary on the whole Bible: Wherein each chapter is summed up in its contents: The sacred text inserted at large in distinct paragraphs ; each paragraph reduced to its proper heads: The sense given, and largely illustrated with practical remarks and observations* (Vol. 6). F.H. Revell.

Jamieson, R. (n.d.). *Galatians.* Robert Jamieson: Commentary critical and explanatory on the whole Bible - christian classics ethereal library. https://ccel.org/ccel/jamieson/jfb/jfb.xi.ix.vii.html

Jamieson, R., Fausset, A. R., & Brown, D. (2008). *A Commentary on the Old and New Testaments* (Vol. 3). Hendrickson Publishers.

Lindner, P. (2003). Power bible CD Version (3.9). *Power Bible*. Retrieved June 27, 2023, from https://powerbible.com/.

Nichols, M. (2007, December 26). *Paris loses out: Hilton Fortune pledged to charity.* Reuters. https://www.reuters.com/article/uk-hilton-charity/paris-loses-out-hilton-fortune-pledged-to-charity-idUKN2636653220071226

Nomani, A. Q. (2022, December 25). *Top us school hides student academic awards to not hurt people's.* News.com. https://www.news.com.au/lifestyle/parenting/school-life/top-us-school-hides-student-academic-awards-to-not-hurt-peoples-feelings/news-story/e6fceef07f05ae466800622378c7cac6

Pfeiffer, C. F., Carlson, E. L., & Scharlemann, M. H. (2003). *Baker's Bible Atlas*. Baker Book House.

Search tools. The Institute for Creation Research. (n.d.). https://www.icr.org/bible/Galatians/3/11

Wright, D. (2015, July 15). *How long were the Israelites in Egypt?* Answers in Genesis. https://answersingenesis.org/bible-questions/how-long-were-the-israelites-in-egypt

Yglesias, M. (2016, January 6). *What does all the land in Manhattan cost?* Vox. https://www.vox.com/2016/1/6/10719304/manhattan-land-value

Other Books by Dr. Wagner

Daniel: Breathtaking
Esther: Five Feasts and the Fingerprints of God
James: The Pen and the Plumb Line
Jonah: A Story of Greatness
Nehemiah: A Labor of Love
Proverbs Vol 1: Bright Light from Dark Sayings
Proverbs Vol 2: Bright Light from Dark Sayings
The Revelation: Ready or Not
Romans: Salvation from A-Z
Ruth: Diamonds in the Darkness

Beyond the Colored Coat
From Footers to Finish Nails
Learning Not to Fear the Old Testament
Marriage Makers/Marriage Breakers
I'm Saved! Now What???
Don't Muzzle the Ox

Books in the Night Heroes Series

Cry from the Coal Mine (Vol 1)
Free Fall (Vol 2)
Broken Brotherhood (Vol 3)
The Blade of Black Crow (Vol 4)
Ghost Ship (Vol 5)
When Serpents Rise (Vol 6)
Moth Man (Vol 7)
Runaway (Vol 8)
Terror by Day (Vol 9)
Winter Wolf (Vol 10)
Desert Heat (Vol 11)

Other Fiction

Zak Blue: Falcon Wing
Zak Blue: Enter the Maelstrom

Devotionals

DO Drops Vol. 1
DO Drops Vol. 2
DO Drops Vol. 3
DO Drops Vol. 4
DO Drops Vol. 5
DO Drops Vol. 6
DO Drops Vol. 7
DO Drops Vol. 8
DO Drops Vol. 9

www.ingramcontent.com/pod-product-compliance
Lightning Source LLC
Chambersburg PA
CBHW072005040426
42447CB00009B/1493